Healthy Meals for Lowering Blood Pressure: Delicious DASH Diet Recipes

Charly .D Horner

Healthy Meals for Lowering Blood Pressure: Delicious DASH Diet Recipes : Discover Easy and Tasty Dishes to Lower High Blood Pressure Naturally

Funny helpful tips:

Practice gratitude; focus on the positives in your relationship.

Life's symphony is a melody of moments; savor each note, for it adds depth to your song.

Life advices:

In the universe of experiences, seek out opportunities that align with your soul's desires.

Practice critical reading; question the author's intent and evaluate the content's validity.

Introduction

This is a valuable resource designed to introduce individuals to the Dietary Approaches to Stop Hypertension (DASH) diet.

This guide focuses on the potential benefits of the DASH diet, such as lowering blood pressure and reducing cholesterol levels. It goes beyond typical recipe collections by incorporating practical tips and tricks for effective fat burning while following the DASH diet.

The cookbook begins by explaining the fundamental principles of the DASH diet and its positive impact on cardiovascular health. It emphasizes user-friendly tips and tricks, making it accessible for beginners. The guide provides insights into the connection between the DASH diet and weight loss, catering to those seeking both heart health and effective weight management.

Organized into various sections, the cookbook features a diverse range of recipes suitable for different preferences and dietary needs. These sections cover a wide array of meal categories, ensuring there are options for breakfast, brunch, appetizers, snacks, fish, seafood, salads, poultry, soups, stews, curries, pasta, noodles, vegetables, leafy greens, desserts, and smoothies.

The recipes are crafted to align with the DASH diet principles, offering nutritious and flavorful options. Each section caters to different tastes and dietary preferences, providing a comprehensive collection for individuals looking to adopt a heart-healthy lifestyle. Additionally, the cookbook includes a 30-day meal plan to assist those seeking a structured approach to transitioning to the DASH diet.

In summary, this book serves as a practical and informative resource, offering a diverse array of recipes and insights to support individuals in embracing the DASH diet for improved cardiovascular health and overall well-being.

Contents

WHAT IS THE DASH DIET?

DASH (Dietary Approaches to Stop Hypertension) is a healthy eating strategy intended to help treat or prevent high blood pressure.

The diet's foundations are as follows:
A.   Consume more veggies, fruits, and low-fat dairy products.
B.   Reduce your intake of foods high in saturated fat, cholesterol, and trans fats.
C.   Increase your intake of whole grains, poultry, fish, and nuts.
D.   Reduce your intake of red meat, sweets, sugary drinks, and sodium.
E.   Restrict foods high in saturated fats (e.g., oils and full-fat dairy).
F.   Limit alcohol consumption.

You can determine how many calories you should consume each day with the aid of your healthcare expert. Your calorie requirements will depend on your age, sex, the amount of exercise you regularly partake in, health issues, and whether you're attempting to maintain or lose weight.

HOW DOES THE DASH DIET LOWER BLOOD PRESSURE & REDUCE CHOLESTEROL?

The DASH Diet & Blood Pressure

The DASH diet has an emphasis on fiber-rich meals, as well as foods high in calcium, potassium, and magnesium, all of which work together to decrease blood pressure. Foods that are heavy in sodium, saturated fats, and added sugars are restricted.

The DASH Diet & Cholesterol

Getting plenty of fiber—in this case, from fruits, vegetables, whole grains, nuts, and beans—eating fish and lean cuts of meat, and avoiding sugar and refined carbohydrates are all components of the DASH diet, which has been associated with lower cholesterol levels.

The DASH diet improves LDL and total cholesterol in both their higher-fat and conventional forms, but the higher-fat variants raise HDL (i.e., "good" cholesterol).

EASY TIPS & TRICKS TO BURN FAT ON THE DASH DIET

DASH Diet Tips & Tricks

1. Add veggies to your supper and lunch menus.
2. Add a portion of fruit to your meals.
3. Use low-fat or fat-free condiments and less butter, margarine, and salad dressing.
4. Drink low-fat or skim dairy products.
5. Create vegetarian dishes.
6. Increase your intake of dry beans and veggies.
7. Snack on unsalted pretzels, nuts, raisins, low-fat and fat-free yogurt, frozen yogurt, unsalted popcorn without butter, and raw veggies, rather than chips or sweets.
8. Always read food labels and choose items with less salt.

How to Lose Weight with the DASH Diet

Keep a Food Diary/Log

Make a list of your present daily eating habits. Every meal of the day should be noted on paper, along with the meals you skip. Be sure to note if you frequently forget to have breakfast. Even if you eat snacks idly (e.g., while watching TV), note them down, as well. You can use this journal to track your eating habits over time and identify areas where adjustments might be made.

Calculate Your Caloric Needs

To do this, determine your degree of physical activity. If you want to lose weight, then you must consume fewer calories than you expend or maintain an active lifestyle to burn more calories than you consume.

Transition to the DASH Diet Gradually

Too many changes at once might be unsettling and make you want to backslide, which can result in a total relapse. Instead, pace yourself as you modify your diet, and you won't even notice the change; you'll just reap the health benefits.

Get Enough Rest & Sleep

It has been demonstrated that adhering to a regular sleep pattern and getting roughly eight hours of sleep per day helps maintain a lower proportion of body fat and encourages general wellness.

Don't Follow Fad Diets

Fad diets make weight-loss promises and frequently imply that you can lose weight without exercising by consuming an unbalanced, unhealthy diet. These diets carry significant health hazards. Examples of fad diets include liquid diets, juice fasts, and grapefruit diets.

Replace Unhealthy Snacks with Fruit

Studies have demonstrated that having fruit close at hand and harmful treats out of reach promotes healthier eating habits. So, whenever you want cookies, try eating a medium-sized apple instead. You'll successfully satiate your hunger and support weight loss.

Consume Fewer Servings

Studies have demonstrated that spreading out your daily meals into smaller portions helps you lose weight. So, if you're craving a hamburger, then go ahead and indulge; not doing so will just make you unhappy. However, make the burger three ounces in size, rather than six ounces.

BREAKFAST & BRUNCH RECIPES

BREAKFAST & BRUNCH RECIPES

Nut & Seed Granola

SERVINGS: 2
COOKING TIME: 40 MINUTES
DIFFICULTY: EASY

INGREDIENTS:
• ¼ cup sunflower seeds, shelled
• 1 cup cashews
• 1 pinch salt substitute
• ¼ cup pumpkin seeds, shelled
• ¾ cup almonds
• ½ cup unsweetened coconut flakes
• A few drops of stevia
• 1 teaspoon vanilla

INSTRUCTIONS:
1. Preheat your oven to 300 degrees F and line a baking sheet.
2. Blend the cashews, almonds, coconut flakes, and pumpkin seeds.
3. In a bowl, combine vanilla and stevia together.
4. Add the blended mixture and the sunflower seeds; stir to coat.
5. Spread the mixture onto the baking sheet and bake for 25 minutes.
6. Remove from heat.
7. Add the salt substitute.
8. Break into pieces when it is cool enough to handle.

NUTRITION:
Calories: 85 | Protein: 4.4 g | Fat: 1.9 g | Carbohydrates: 26 g | Sodium: 97 mg

Vegan Parmesan & Spinach Frittata

SERVINGS: 4
COOKING TIME: 12 MINUTES
DIFFICULTY: EASY

INGREDIENTS:
• 2 tablespoons olive oil
• ½ teaspoons salt
• 2 cups fresh baby spinach
• 8 eggs, beaten
• ⅛ teaspoon black pepper
• 2 tablespoons grated vegan parmesan
• 1 teaspoon garlic powder

INSTRUCTIONS:
1. Preheat the grill.
2. In a skillet, heat the olive oil.
3. Add the spinach to the skillet and cook, stirring periodically, for about three minutes.
4. Combine the eggs, garlic powder, salt, and black pepper in a bowl. Pour over the spinach and simmer for three minutes.
5. Scrape the eggs from the pan's edge gently with a rubber spatula.
6. Place the pan under the broiler and top with vegan parmesan cheese.
7. Bake for three minutes until the edges are golden brown.
8. Cut into pieces to serve.

NUTRITION:
Calories: 203 | Fat: 12 g | Carbohydrates: 23 g | Fiber: 6 g | Protein: 15 g | Sodium: 238 mg

Chickpea & Flax Seed Tortillas

SERVINGS: 4
COOKING TIME: 20 MINUTES
DIFFICULTY: MODERATE

INGREDIENTS:
• 2 tablespoons ground flax seeds
• 2 tablespoons lukewarm water
• 1 cup chickpea flour
• 1 cup water
• 1 pinch sea salt
• 1 pinch turmeric
• 1 pinch cumin

INSTRUCTIONS (FOR EACH TORTILLA):
1. Combine flax seeds and lukewarm water in a bowl.
2. Let sit for 5-10 minutes to thicken until it comes together.
3. Preheat the skillet.
4. Pour in 1/2 cup batter and stir to coat the bottom.
5. Cook the first side for about three minutes.
6. Flip and cook for another minute.

NUTRITION:
Calories: 80 | Fat: 2 g | Carbohydrates: 11.7 g | Fiber: 3.9 g | Protein: 4 g | Sodium: 110 mg

DASH Diet-Friendly Pumpkin Waffles

SERVINGS: 4
COOKING TIME: 20 MINUTES
DIFFICULTY: EASY

INGREDIENTS:
- ½ cup almond flour
- ½ cup coconut flour
- 1 teaspoon baking powder
- 1½ teaspoons ground cinnamon
- ¾ teaspoon ground ginger
- ½ teaspoon ground cloves
- ½ teaspoon ground nutmeg
- 2 tablespoons olive oil
- 5 organic eggs
- ¾ cup almond milk
- ½ cup pumpkin purée
- 2 bananas, peeled and sliced
- 1 pinch salt substitute

INSTRUCTIONS:
1. Preheat the waffle maker, then grease it.
2. Blend all ingredients until thoroughly combined.
3. Pour into waffle maker and cook for about five minutes.

NUTRITION:
Calories: 129 | Fat: 9.5 g | Carbohydrates: 31 g | Fiber: 10.8 g | Protein: 14.1 g | Sodium: 170 mg

Golden Flax & Chia

SERVINGS: 2
COOKING TIME: 120 MINUTES
DIFFICULTY: HARD

INGREDIENTS:
• 2 tablespoons almond oil, melted
• ½ cup golden Flax-Meal
• ½ cup Chia seed
• 2 tablespoons dark ground cinnamon
• 1 tablespoons hemp protein powder
• A few drops of stevia
• 1 teaspoon vanilla extract
• ¾ cup hot water

INSTRUCTIONS:
1. Combine all ingredients.
2. Spread the dough into a thin layer onto a parchment paper-lined cookie sheet.
3. Bake at 325 degrees F for 15 minutes, then cut into pieces.
4. Lower the temperature to 300 degrees F and let set for 30 minutes.
5. Remove and separate the pieces.
6. Bake the pieces at 200 degrees F for one hour.
7. Enjoy!

NUTRITION:
Calories: 131 | Sodium: 85 mg | Carbohydrates: 12 g | Fiber: 12 g | Sugars: 3 g | Protein: 19 g

Apple Chia Delight

SERVINGS: 2
COOKING TIME: 15 MINUTES
DIFFICULTY: EASY

INGREDIENTS:
- ½ chopped dried organic apple
- 2 cups organic chia seeds
- 1 cup organic hemp hearts
- 2 tablespoons real cinnamon
- 1 cup chopped nuts
- 1 teaspoon low sodium salt

INSTRUCTIONS:
1. Combine everything.
2. Serve with a few drops of stevia.

NUTRITION:
Calories: 83 | Protein: 4.8 g | Carbohydrates: 18 g | Fiber: 11 g | Sugars: 7 g | Fat: 2.7 g | Sodium: 93 mg

Apple, Almond & Coconut Bowl

SERVINGS: 2
COOKING TIME: 10 MINUTES
DIFFICULTY: EASY

INGREDIENTS:
- ½ apple cored and roughly diced
- 1 pinch of cinnamon
- 2 Tablespoons sliced almonds
- 2 Tablespoons of unsweetened coconut
- 1 pinch of low sodium salt

INSTRUCTIONS:
1. Pulse everything in the food processor.
2. Serve with nut milk.

NUTRITION:
Calories: 68 | Fat: 1.2 g | Sodium: 145 mg | Carbohydrates: 12 g | Sugars: 2 g | Fiber: 14 g | Protein: 5 g

Paleo Porridge with Banana

SERVINGS: 2
COOKING TIME: 15 MINUTES
DIFFICULTY: EASY

INGREDIENTS:
- ½ cup soaked pecans
- ¾ cup boiling water
- 2 tablespoons coconut butter
- ½ very ripe banana
- A few drops of stevia
- ½ teaspoon cinnamon
- ⅛ teaspoon sea salt

INSTRUCTIONS:
1. Blend all of the ingredients in a food processor.
2. Transfer to a saucepan and heat gently until thick and creamy.

NUTRITION:
Calories: 110 | Fat: 1.9 g | Sodium: 156 mg | Carbohydrates: 19 g | Sugars: 15 g | Protein: 8 g

Raisin & Nut Breakfast Cereal

SERVINGS: 2
COOKING TIME: 15 MINUTES
DIFFICULTY: MODERATE

INGREDIENTS:
• 1 cup almonds, chopped
• ½ cup sunflower seeds
• ½ cup almond meal
• ¼ cup pumpkin seeds
• 2 cups coconut
• 1½ teaspoon cinnamon
• 1 cup raisins
• 3 tablespoons almond oil
• 2 tablespoons squash seeds
• ¼ cup raw honey
• 1 teaspoon vanilla

INSTRUCTIONS:
1. Preheat the oven to 325 degrees F.
2. Mix all ingredients, except raisins, in a bowl.
3. Heat almond oil, vanilla and honey and pour over dry ingredients; combine well.
4. Spread on a pan and bake at 325 degrees F for 26 minutes, stirring halfway through.
5. Cool. Add raisins and serve with home-made coconut milk or home-made almond milk! Store in an airtight container.

NUTRITION:
Calories: 120 | Fat: 3 g | Carbohydrates: 40 g | Fiber: 19 g | Sugars: 8 g | Protein: 4 g | Sodium: 113 mg

Cinnamon Chia Pudding

SERVINGS: 4
COOKING TIME: 25 MINUTES
DIFFICULTY: EASY

INGREDIENTS:
- ½ cup chia seeds
- 1½ cups almond milk
- ½ cup pumpkin purée
- 1 pinch of salt
- 2 tablespoons of raw honey
- ⅛ teaspoon cloves
- 2 tablespoons almond butter
- 1 teaspoon vanilla extract
- 1 protein powder sachet
- ¼ teaspoon nutmeg powder
- 1 teaspoon cinnamon powder
- ⅛ teaspoon ginger

INSTRUCTIONS:
1. Blend all of the ingredients, except the chia seeds.
2. Add the chia seeds and mix well.
3. Refrigerate overnight before serving.

NUTRITION:
Calories: 135 | Fat: 2 g | Carbohydrates: 32 g | Fiber: 9 g | Sugars: 12 g | Protein: 11 g | Sodium: 123 mg

Oatmeal with Coconut Milk

SERVINGS: 2
COOKING TIME: 25 MINUTES
DIFFICULTY: EASY

INGREDIENTS:
- ¾ cup unsweetened coconut milk
- ½ cup gluten-free quick-cooking rolled oats
- ½ teaspoon ground cinnamon
- ½ teaspoon ground turmeric
- ¼ teaspoon ground ginger

INSTRUCTIONS:
1. Combine milk and oats and microwave for about 1 minute.
2. Mix in the spices and microwave for another 2 minutes.
3. Serve with a garnish of your choice.

NUTRITION:
Calories: 121 | Fat: 2 g | Carbohydrates: 17 g | Fiber: 3 g | Sugars: 7.5 g | Protein: 6 g | Sodium: 95 mg

Walnut Porridge

SERVINGS: 4
COOKING TIME: 40 MINUTES
DIFFICULTY: EASY

INGREDIENTS:
• ½ cup pecans
• ½ cup almonds
• ¼ cup sunflower seeds
• ¼ cup chia seeds
• ¼ cup unsweetened coconut flakes
• 4 cups unsweetened almond milk
• ½ teaspoon cinnamon powder
• ¼ teaspoon ginger powder
• 1 teaspoon powdered stevia
• 1 tablespoon almond butter

INSTRUCTIONS:
1. Blend pecans, almonds, and sunflower seeds in a food processor.
2. In a skillet, add the nut mix, chia seeds, coconut flakes, almond milk, spices, and stevia and bring to a gentle boil; simmer for 20 minutes.
3. Serve with a dollop of almond butter.

NUTRITION:
Calories: 142 | Fat: 2 g | Carbohydrates: 12 g | Fiber: 7.5 g | Sugars: 1.2 g | Protein: 8 g | Sodium: 121 mg

DASH Diet-Friendly Apple Omelet

SERVINGS: 1
COOKING TIME: 20 MINUTES
DIFFICULTY: EASY

INGREDIENTS:
• 2 teaspoons almond oil
• ½ green apple, cored and thinly sliced
• ¼ teaspoon ground cinnamon
• ⅛ teaspoon ground nutmeg
• 2 organic eggs
• ⅛ teaspoon organic vanilla extract
• 1 pinch of salt

INSTRUCTIONS:
1. In a non-stick skillet, melt 1 teaspoon almond oil and sauté the apple slices with the nutmeg and cinnamon for about 5 minutes, turning once halfway through.
2. Put the eggs, vanilla, and salt in a bowl and beat until fluffy.
3. Melt the remaining oil in a pan and cook the egg mixture for about 4 minutes.
4. Invert the pan onto a platter and fold the omelet in half.

NUTRITION:
Calories: 164| Fat: 9 g | Carbohydrates: 19 g | Fiber: 3.1 g | Sugars: 2.5 g | Protein: 13 g | Sodium: 93 mg

Quinoa Porridge

SERVINGS: 4
COOKING TIME: 25 MINUTES
DIFFICULTY: MODERATE

INGREDIENTS:
• 2 cups of water
• ½ teaspoon organic vanilla extract
• ½ cup coconut milk
• 1 cup uncooked red quinoa, rinsed and drained
• ¼ teaspoon fresh lemon zest, finely grated
• 10-12 drops of liquid stevia
• 1 teaspoon ground cinnamon
• ½ teaspoon ground ginger
• ½ teaspoon ground nutmeg
• 1 pinch of ground cloves
• 2 tablespoons almonds, chopped

INSTRUCTIONS:
1. Mix quinoa, water, and vanilla extract in a skillet and bring to a boil.
2. Reduce to low heat and simmer for about 15 minutes.
3. Add the coconut milk, lemon zest, stevia, and spices to the skillet with the quinoa and stir.
4. Remove the quinoa from the heat and fluff it with a fork right away.
5. Divide the quinoa mixture evenly among serving bowls.
6. Serve with a garnish of chopped almonds.

NUTRITION:
Calories: 88 | Fat: 2.4 g | Carbohydrates: 27 g | Fiber: 14 g | Sugars: 3 g | Protein: 7.4 g | Sodium: 65 mg

Sugar-Free Protein Muesli

SERVINGS: 2
COOKING TIME: 15 MINUTES
DIFFICULTY: EASY

INGREDIENTS:
- ½ teaspoon cinnamon
- 1 cup unsweetened unsulfured coconut flakes
- 1 tablespoon chopped walnuts
- 1 scoop of hemp protein
- 1 tablespoon raw almonds
- 1 tablespoon dark and sugar-free chocolate chips
- 1 cup unsweetened almond milk

INSTRUCTIONS:
1. Layer coconut flakes, walnuts, almonds, and chocolate chips in a bowl.
2. Sprinkle with cinnamon and drizzle almond milk over the muesli.

NUTRITION:
Calories: 83 | Fat: 1.2 g | Carbohydrates: 24 g | Fiber: 15 g | Protein: 11 g | Sodium: 68 mg

Pork Cracklings with Eggs

SERVINGS: 3
COOKING TIME: 20 MINUTES
DIFFICULTY: MODERATE

INGREDIENTS:
• 4 slices Bacon, cooked
• 5 Eggs
• 5 oz. Pork Rinds
• 1 Tomato
• ¼ cup Cilantro, chopped
• 1 Avocado
• 2 Jalapeño Peppers, de-seeded
• 1 Onion
• Salt and Pepper to taste

INSTRUCTIONS:
1. In the bacon fat, fry pork rinds.
2. Add the vegetables to the skillet once the pig rinds are crispy.
3. Add chopped cilantro to the pan once the onions are almost transparent.
4. Mix everything in the pan with 5 pre-scrambled eggs.
5. Season with salt and pepper as needed.
6. Cook like an omelet.
7. Just before serving, dice an avocado and fold it into the mixture.

NUTRITION:
Calories: 221 | Fat: 14 g | Carbohydrates: 25 g | Protein: 27 g | Sodium: 188 mg

Italian Pizza Waffles

SERVINGS: 2
COOKING TIME: 15 MINUTES
DIFFICULTY: EXPERT

INGREDIENTS:
• 4 Eggs
• 1 teaspoon Italian Seasoning
• 4 tablespoons Parmesan Cheese
• 3 tablespoons Almond Flour
• 1 tablespoon Bacon Grease
• 1 tablespoon Psyllium Husk Powder
• Salt and Pepper to Taste
• ½ cup Tomato Sauce
• 1 teaspoon Baking Powder
• 3 oz. Cheddar Cheese
• 14 slices Pepperoni

INSTRUCTIONS:
1. In a container, combine all ingredients, excluding tomato sauce and cheese, using an immersion blender.
2. Preheat your waffle iron and pour half of the batter into it.
3. Allow cooking for a few minutes.
4. Top each waffle with tomato sauce and cheese.
5. Then, in the oven, broil for 4 minutes.
6. Add pepperoni on the top of them if desired.

NUTRITION:
Calories: 216 | Fat: 7 g | Carbohydrates: 75 g | Sodium: 292 mg | Protein: 14 g

Nutmeg-Spiced Quinoa Porridge

SERVINGS: 4
COOKING TIME: 25 MINUTES
DIFFICULTY: EASY

INGREDIENTS:
- 1 pinch of ground cloves
- 2 cups of water
- 1 cup red quinoa, cooked
- ½ teaspoon ground ginger
- ½ teaspoon vanilla extract
- ½ cup coconut milk
- ¼ teaspoon fresh lemon zest, finely grated
- 10-12 drops of liquid stevia
- 1 teaspoon ground cinnamon
- ½ teaspoon ground nutmeg
- 2 tablespoons almonds, chopped

INSTRUCTIONS:
1. Combine quinoa and vanilla extract.
2. Add the coconut milk, lemon zest, stevia, and spices to a skillet with the quinoa and stir.
3. Fluff quinoa with a fork.
4. Divide the quinoa mixture evenly among serving bowls.
5. Serve with a garnish of chopped almonds.

NUTRITION:
Calories: 98 | Fat: 2 g | Carbohydrates: 21 g | Fiber: 16 g | Sugars: 1.3 g | Protein: 8.4 g | Sodium: 245 mg

Protein Almond Muesli

SERVINGS: 2
COOKING TIME: 10 MINUTES
DIFFICULTY: EASY

INGREDIENTS:
- ½ teaspoon cinnamon
- 1 tablespoon raw almonds
- 1 cup unsweetened unsulfured coconut flakes
- 1 tablespoon chopped walnuts
- 1 tablespoon dark no-sugar-added chocolate chips
- 1 cup unsweetened almond milk
- 1 scoop of hemp protein

INSTRUCTIONS:
1. Toss together the coconut flakes, walnuts, almonds, and chocolate chips in a medium mixing bowl.
2. Sprinkle cinnamon on top.
3. Douse the muesli with cold almond milk and devour with a spoon.

NUTRITION:
Calories: 109 | Fat: 3 g | Carbohydrates: 21 g | Sodium: 191 mg | Sugars: 4 g | Fiber: 12 g | Protein: 23 g

Apple-Cinnamon Chia

SERVINGS: 2
COOKING TIME: 10 MINUTES
DIFFICULTY: EASY

INGREDIENTS:
- ½ chopped dried apple
- 2 cups chia seeds
- 1 cup hemp hearts
- 2 tablespoons real cinnamon
- 1 teaspoon salt substitute
- ½ tablespoon chopped nuts of your choice

INSTRUCTIONS:
1. Combine all ingredients.
2. Add a few drops of stevia to each serving.

NUTRITION:
Calories: 73 | Protein: 4.8 g | Carbohydrates: 15 g | Fiber: 11 g | Sodium: 97 mg | Sugars: 8 g | Fat: 1.7 g

Apple Almond Coconut Bowl

SERVINGS: 2
COOKING TIME: 10 MINUTES
DIFFICULTY: EASY

INGREDIENTS:
- 1 pinch of cinnamon
- ½ apple, cored and roughly diced
- 1 handful of sliced almonds
- 1 handful of unsweetened coconut
- 1 pinch of salt substitute

INSTRUCTIONS:
1. Combine all ingredients.
2. Add a few drops of stevia to each serving.

NUTRITION:
Calories: 71 | Fat: 1.2 g | Sodium: 95 mg | Carbohydrates: 12 g |
Sugars: 8 g | Fiber: 12 g | Protein: 4 g

Pecan Porridge with Banana

SERVINGS: 2
COOKING TIME: 10 MINUTES
DIFFICULTY: EASY

INGREDIENTS:
- ½ cup soaked pecans
- ¾ cup boiling water
- ½ very ripe banana
- A few drops of stevia
- 2 tablespoons coconut butter
- ½ teaspoon cinnamon
- ⅛ teaspoon sea salt

INSTRUCTIONS:
1. Blend everything until smooth and creamy.
2. Cook the mixture in a pan for about 5 minutes.

NUTRITION:
Calories: 130 | Fat: 29 g | Sodium: 168 mg | Carbohydrates: 23 g |
Sugars: 7 g | Protein: 6 g

Spicy Sweet Potato Breakfast Bowl

SERVINGS: 4
COOKING TIME: 40 MINUTES
DIFFICULTY: HARD

INGREDIENTS:
- 2 sweet potatoes, peeled and diced
- 1 pinch salt substitute
- 1 pinch black pepper
- ½ bell pepper, diced
- 1 teaspoon chili powder
- ½ onion, diced
- ½ tablespoon extra virgin olive oil
- 1 jalapeño, chopped
- 2-3 cups fresh spinach
- 2 eggs
- ½ red bell pepper, diced
- 1 avocado, sliced
- 1 teaspoon ghee
- 2 strips bacon, cooked and crumbled

INSTRUCTIONS:
1. Preheat the oven to 375 degrees Fahrenheit.
2. Toss diced sweet potatoes with extra virgin olive oil, salt substitute, black pepper, and chili powder on a lined baking pan.
3. Bake for 20 minutes, rotating halfway through.
4. Sauté the onion, bell peppers, and jalapeño in a skillet for 6 minutes or until tender.
5. Add the spinach and cook until tender.
6. In a separate skillet, melt the ghee. Cook the eggs until thickened, seasoning with salt substitute and black pepper.
7. Place the sweet potatoes in two separate dishes.
8. Top with vegetable mixture, followed by the eggs, bacon, and

avocado.

NUTRITION:
Calories: 235 | Fat: 15 g | Sodium: 443 mg | Carbohydrates: 27 g | Fiber: 4 g | Sugars: 2g | Protein: 28 g

Blueberry Cinnamon Breakfast Bake

SERVINGS: 4
COOKING TIME: 40 MINUTES
DIFFICULTY: MODERATE

INGREDIENTS:
• 2 teaspoons cinnamon, divided
• 2 eggs, beaten
• ¼ cup brown sugar, divided
• 8 slices of whole-wheat bread
• 1 cup of low-fat milk
• 3 cups blueberries
• Zest of 1 lemon, divided

INSTRUCTIONS:
1. Preheat the oven to 350 degrees F.
2. Mix cinnamon, eggs, milk, brown sugar, and zest in a bowl.
3. In a mixing bowl, toss the bread and blueberries with the egg mixture and whisk until most of the liquid has been absorbed.
4. Pour batter into muffin tins.
5. Sprinkle 1 tablespoon brown sugar and 1 teaspoon cinnamon over the French toast cups.
6. Cook for 18 minutes, or until the French toast is done and the top is browned.
7. In a small saucepan, combine the remaining 1 cup of blueberries, lemon zest, and 1 tablespoon brown sugar and cook for 10 minutes, or until liquid is released.
8. Crush blueberries and dollop the syrupy blueberry over the toasted French toast.

NUTRITION:
Calories: 210 | Fat: 5 g | Sodium: 171 mg | Carbohydrates: 29 g | Fiber: 4 g | Sugars: 3 g | Protein: 13 g

Cinnamon Quinoa with Peach & Pecan

SERVINGS: 4
COOKING TIME: 15 MINUTES
DIFFICULTY: EASY

INGREDIENTS:
• Cooking spray
• 2½ cups water
• ½ teaspoon ground cinnamon
• 2 cups frozen, unsweetened peach slices
• 1½ cups fat-free half-and-half
• 1 cup uncooked quinoa, rinsed, drained
• ¼ cup sugar
• 1½ teaspoons vanilla extract
• ¼ cup chopped pecans, dry-roasted

INSTRUCTIONS:
1. Add some water to oiled slow cooker.
2. In a mixing dish, combine the quinoa and cinnamon.
3. Cook for 2 hours on low, or until the quinoa is mushy and the water has been absorbed.
4. Just before serving the quinoa, mix the half-and-half, sugar, and vanilla essence in a separate dish until the sugar has dissolved.
5. Place the quinoa into dishes to serve. On top of that, place the peaches. Mix the half-and-half and pour it in.
6. Garnish with pecans.

NUTRITION:
Calories: 109 | Fat: 3 g | Sodium: 95 mg | Carbohydrate: 24 g | Protein: 12 g

Quick Oats with Coconut Milk

SERVINGS: 2
COOKING TIME: 15 MINUTES
DIFFICULTY: EASY

INGREDIENTS:
• ¾ cup unsweetened coconut milk
• ½ cup gluten-free quick-cooking rolled oats
• ½ teaspoon ground cinnamon
• ½ teaspoon ground turmeric
• ¼ teaspoon ground ginger

INSTRUCTIONS:
1. In a microwave-safe bowl, combine milk and oats and microwave on high for about 45 seconds.
2. Mix in the spices.
3. Microwave for 2 minutes, stirring after 20 seconds.

NUTRITION:
Calories: 91| Fat: 1.2 g | Carbohydrates: 17 g | Fiber: 18 g | Sodium: 70 mg | Sugars: 3.5 g | Protein: 6 g

Walnut and Almond Porridge

SERVINGS: 4
COOKING TIME: 40 MINUTES
DIFFICULTY: EASY

INGREDIENTS:
- ½ cup pecans
- ½ cup almonds
- ¼ cup sunflower seeds
- ¼ cup chia seeds
- ¼ cup coconut flakes(unsweetened)
- 4 cups almond milk(unsweetened)
- ½ teaspoon cinnamon powder
- ¼ teaspoon ginger powder
- 1 teaspoon powdered stevia
- 1 tablespoon almond butter

INSTRUCTIONS:
1. In a food processor, combine pecans, almonds, and sunflower seeds.
2. Bring the nut mixture, chia seeds, coconut flakes, almond milk, spices, and stevia powder to a boil for about 20 minutes.
3. Serve with a dollop of almond butter.

NUTRITION:
Calories: 112 | Fat: 1.5 g | Carbohydrates: 16 g | Fiber: 15 g | Sodium: 96 mg | Sugars: 4 g | Protein: 12 g

Cinnamon Millet Porridge

SERVINGS: 4
COOKING TIME: 20 MINUTES
DIFFICULTY: MODERATE

INGREDIENTS:
- 2 teaspoons ground cinnamon
- ½ teaspoon ground cloves
- 1 tablespoon coconut butter
- 1½ cups finely ground millet
- 1½ cups of water
- 1 teaspoon ginger powder
- 4 cups unsweetened coconut milk

INSTRUCTIONS:
1. In a skillet over medium-high heat, melt the coconut oil and brown the spices for about 30 seconds.
2. Add millet and stir to combine.
3. Bring the water and coconut milk to a boil, stirring constantly.
4. Simmer for about 15 minutes.
5. Serve with desired garnish.

NUTRITION:
Calories: 98| Fat: 1.5 g | Carbohydrates: 23 g | Fiber: 12 g | Sugars: 6 g | Protein: 14 g | Sodium: 127 mg

APPETIZER & SNACK RECIPES

APPETIZER & SNACK RECIPES

Tofu and Vegetable Skewers

SERVINGS: 4
COOKING TIME: 100 MINUTES
DIFFICULTY: EXPERT

INGREDIENTS:
- 1-pound extra-firm tofu, squeezed dry and cubed
- 16 mushrooms
- 16 bunches of broccoli
- 1 zucchini, sliced
- 2 onions, sliced
- ⅓ cup vegetable broth or water
- 2 tablespoons olive oil or other oil
- 2 bell peppers, diced
- 2 tablespoons agave nectar or maple syrup
- Zest and juice of 1 lime
- 1½ tablespoons of tamari
- 1 tablespoon garlic, crushed
- 1 teaspoon hot sauce
- ¼ teaspoon black pepper, freshly ground
- 1 Tablespoon curry powder
- 1 tablespoon grated ginger

INSTRUCTIONS:
1. Thread each skewer in this order: a mushroom, a piece of orange pepper, a broccoli floret, a cube of tofu, a slice of zucchini, a piece of red pepper, and a new onion. Repeat the process, reversing the order and ending with a mushroom.
2. Layer skewers in a baking dish.
3. For the marinade, place the broth, oil, agave nectar, lime zest and juice, tamari, curry powder, garlic, ginger, hot sauce, and pepper in a bowl and whisk together.
4. Pour marinade over skewers.

5. Cover the mold, place it in the refrigerator, and let the tofu and vegetables marinate for 1 hour or more.
6. Grill the skewers on a hot oiled grill or griddle until the tofu and vegetables are lightly charred, 3 minutes per side.

NUTRITION:
Calories: 153 | Protein: 14 g | Fat: 1.8 g| Carbohydrates: 28 g | Fiber: 13 g | Sodium: 240 mg

DASH Diet-Friendly Freekeh Balls

SERVINGS: 6
COOKING TIME: 90 MINUTES
DIFFICULTY: EXPERT

INGREDIENTS:
- 1 cup uncooked crushed freekeh
- 1 onion, grated
- 2½ cups of water
- 1 potato, grated
- 2 garlic cloves, crushed
- ½ cup parsley, chopped
- ¾ cup plain or Italian breadcrumbs
- ¾ cup Pecorino Romano cheese, grated
- 3 eggs, beaten
- ¼ teaspoon black pepper
- 2 tablespoons olive oil for brushing
- ½ teaspoon of salt

INSTRUCTIONS:
1. Preheat the oven to 400 degrees Fahrenheit.
2. Using parchment paper, line two baking pans.
3. In a saucepan, add water and freekeh.
4. Bring to a boil, and then simmer for 20 minutes at a low temperature.
5. After the freekeh has cooled, combine all of the ingredients, except the olive oil, and chill for at least an hour.
6. Take 1 heaping tablespoon of the mixture and gently form a meatball between your palms.
7. Line each cookie sheet with 13 meatballs each.
8. Flip with a heatproof spatula and cook 10 minutes until golden brown.

NUTRITION:
Calories: 125 | Fat: 4 g | Carbohydrates: 38 g | Fiber: 7 g | Protein: 13 g | Sodium: 125 mg

Cherries, Dates and Apple Bowl

SERVINGS: 4
COOKING TIME: 20 MINUTES
DIFFICULTY: EASY

INGREDIENTS:
• 2 cups frozen cherries, pitted
• 4 dates, pitted and coarsely chopped
• 1 apple, peeled, cored, and chopped
• 1 cup fresh cherries, pitted
• 2 tablespoons of chia seeds

INSTRUCTIONS:
1. Blend cherries and dates until smooth.
2. In a bowl, combine the apple, fresh cherries, and chia seeds.
3. Stir in the cherry sauce.
4. Refrigerate overnight, covered.

NUTRITION:
Calories: 92 | Fat: 1.8 g | Carbohydrates: 18 g | Fiber: 15 g | Sugars: 5 g | Protein: 9 g | Sodium: 94 mg

Vegan Rice Paper Rolls

SERVINGS: 2
COOKING TIME: 20 MINUTES
DIFFICULTY: MODERATE

INGREDIENTS:
• ½ cucumber, cut into matchsticks
• A handful of bean sprouts
• Uncooked Rice paper
• 4 spring onions
• Handful coriander, chopped
• 1 carrot, cut into matchsticks
• Liquid Aminos
• 1 chili

INSTRUCTIONS:
1. Cook the rice paper rolls by soaking them in a big bowl of boiling water until they become flexible.
2. Toss the coriander with the other ingredients in the rice paper wrappers.
3. Roll and dress in Liquid Aminos.

NUTRITION:
Calories: 93 | Protein: 7 g | Carbohydrates: 16 g | Fiber: 11 g | Sugars: 2.1 g | Fat: 1.3 g | Sodium: 108 mg

Bowl of Raspberry and Almond Milk

SERVINGS: 4
COOKING TIME: 15 MINUTES
DIFFICULTY: EASY

INGREDIENTS:
• 1 cup frozen raspberries
• ¼ cup collagen peptides
• ¼ cup MCT oil
• 2 tablespoons of chia seeds
• 1 teaspoon beetroot powder
• 1 teaspoon organic vanilla extract
• 4 drops of liquid stevia
• 1½ cup almond milk, unsweetened

INSTRUCTIONS:
1. Blend all ingredients until smooth.
2. Pour into 3 serving bowls and serve with your favorite garnish.

NUTRITION:
Calories: 68 | Fat: 1.2 g | Carbohydrates: 16 g | Fiber: 12 g |
Sugars: 6 g | Protein: 9 g | Sodium: 60 mg

Easy Blueberry Muffins

SERVINGS: 6
COOKING TIME: 40 MINUTES
DIFFICULTY: EASY

INGREDIENTS:
• 2½ cups almond flour
• 1 tablespoon coconut flour
• ½ teaspoon baking soda
• 3 tablespoons ground cinnamon
• 1 pinch of salt
• 2 organic eggs
• ¼ cup coconut milk
• ¼ cup almond oil
• ¼ cup maple syrup
• 1 tablespoon organic vanilla extract
• 1 cup fresh blueberries

INSTRUCTIONS:
1. Preheat your oven to 350ºF and oil a muffin pan.
2. Combine the dry ingredients (flour, baking soda, 2 tablespoons cinnamon, and salt) in a dish.
3. In a separate bowl, mix the eggs, milk, oil, maple syrup, and vanilla extract.
4. Stir the egg mixture into the flour mixture.
5. Stir in blueberries.
6. Divide mixture evenly into prepared muffin tins and sprinkle evenly with cinnamon.
7. Bake, for about 24 minutes.

NUTRITION:
Calories: 140| Fat: 3 g | Carbohydrates: 48 g | Fiber: 9 g | Sugars: 11 g | Protein: 17 g | Sodium: 235 mg

Tempeh Cabbage Leaf Rolls

SERVINGS: 4
COOKING TIME: 20 MINUTES
DIFFICULTY: MODERATE

INGREDIENTS:
• 8 ounces of tempeh, sliced horizontally for a total of 8 pieces
• 1 tablespoon of tamari
• 1 ¼ cup sauerkraut, drained
• 2 tablespoons olive oil
• 6 tablespoons chipotle and almond mayonnaise
• 4 kale leaves, lower stems trimmed

INSTRUCTIONS:
1. Put the tempeh in a dish.
2. Pour the tamari over the tempeh and set aside for 10 minutes.
3. In a cast-iron or non-stick skillet, add the sauerkraut and 1/2 tablespoon oil and cook, stirring occasionally, until the sauerkraut is dry and lightly browned.
4. In the same skillet, add the tempeh and the remaining oil and cook for 5 minutes, flipping after 3 minutes.
5. To assemble each roll, place 1 cabbage leaf, ribs side up, on a cutting board.
6. Spread 1½ tablespoons of chipotle and almond mayonnaise in the center of the sheet.
7. Top the mayonnaise with 2 pieces of tempeh, ⅓ cup of sauerkraut, and 1 slice of cucumber.
8. Fold the end of the stem and the top edge of the cabbage leaf towards the center.
9. Fold the right side tightly over the filling, then fold and overlap the left side of the sheet.

NUTRITION:

Calories: 112 | Protein: 10 g | Fat: 17 g | Carbohydrates: 21 g | Fiber: 13 g | Sodium: 195 mg

Stuffed Green Peppers

SERVINGS: 6
COOKING TIME: 60 MINUTES
DIFFICULTY: MODERATE

INGREDIENTS:
- 6 green bell peppers, tops removed
- 10 cups water
- 1 pound tofu crumbles
- 1 clove of garlic, pressed
- ¼ white onions, chopped
- ¼ teaspoon sea salt
- Drizzle of soy sauce
- ½ teaspoon chili powder
- ¼ teaspoon black pepper
- 1 cup cooked rice
- 2 cans of stewed tomatoes
- ¼ cup non-fat mozzarella cheese

INSTRUCTIONS:
1. Preheat the oven to 350 degrees Fahrenheit.
2. In a big pot, submerge the peppers in water; boil on low for 8 minutes.
3. In a skillet, cook the tofu crumbles, garlic, diced green pepper, and white onion, and season with salt and pepper.
4. In another pan, combine soy sauce, the chili pepper, rice, and stewed tomatoes; cook for 5 minutes on low.
5. Arrange the peppers in a big dish. Fill each pepper with the tofu and rice mixture.
6. Pour the remaining stewed tomatoes over the peppers and around them.
7. Top with cheese and bake for 18 minutes.

NUTRITION:
Calories: 164| Fat: 5 g | Sodium: 273 mg | Carbohydrates: 34 g | Fiber: 12 g | Protein: 8 g

DASH Diet-Friendly Carrot and Onion Muffins

SERVINGS: 4
COOKING TIME: 40 MINUTES
DIFFICULTY: MODERATE

INGREDIENTS:
- ¾ cup almond flour
- ½ teaspoon baking soda
- ¼ cup whey protein powder
- 2 teaspoons fresh dill, chopped
- 1 pinch of salt
- 4 organic eggs
- 3 tablespoons of lemon juice
- 2 teaspoons of apple cider vinegar
- 2 tablespoons almond oil, melted
- 1 cup coconut butter, softened
- 1 bunch of spring onions, chopped
- 2 carrots, peeled and grated
- ½ cup fresh parsley, chopped

INSTRUCTIONS:
1. Preheat your oven to 350°F and oil a muffin tin.
2. Combine flour, baking soda, protein powder, and salt in a mixing dish.
3. Combine eggs, vinegar, lemon juice, and oil in another bowl.
4. Add the coconut butter and beat until the mixture becomes smooth.
5. Mix the egg mixture into the flour mixture.
6. Stir in the spring onions, carrots, and parsley.
7. Scoop into the muffin cups and bake for 20 minutes.
8. Invert the muffins onto a serving plate, and serve warm.

NUTRITION:

Calories: 190| Fat: 3 g | Carbohydrates: 29 g | Fiber: 15 g | Sugars: 2 g | Protein: 13 g | Sodium: 121 mg

Neapolitan Bombs

SERVINGS: 12
COOKING TIME: 120 MINUTES
DIFFICULTY: EXPERT

INGREDIENTS:
- ½ cup butter
- ½ cup Cream Cheese
- 2 tablespoons Erythritol
- ½ cup Coconut Oil
- 2 Strawberries
- 25 drops of Liquid Stevia
- 2 tablespoons Cocoa Powder
- 1 teaspoon Vanilla Extract
- ½ cup Sour Cream

INSTRUCTIONS:
1. Blend the butter, coconut oil, sour cream, cream cheese, erythritol, and stevia in an immersion blender until smooth.
2. Separate the mixture into three bowls. Toss the cocoa powder in one bowl, the strawberries in another, and the vanilla in the third.
3. Using an immersion blender, combine all of the ingredients once more. Pour the chocolate mixture into a spout-equipped container.
4. Fill a fat bomb mold halfway with the chocolate mixture. Freeze for 30 minutes before repeating with the vanilla mixture.
5. Freeze for at least 30 minutes.
6. Remove them from the fat bomb molds once they've totally frozen.

NUTRITION:
175 Calories | Fat: 7 g | Carbohydrates: 21 g | Protein: 3 g | Sodium: 258 mg

Rotisserie Chicken Pizza

SERVINGS: 4
COOKING TIME: 25 MINUTES
DIFFICULTY: EASY

INGREDIENTS:
DAIRY-FREE PIZZA CRUST
• 6 Eggs
• 6 tablespoons Parmesan Cheese, shredded
• 3 tablespoons Psyllium Husk Powder
• 1½ teaspoon Italian Seasoning
• Salt and Pepper to Taste
TOPPINGS
• 4 oz. Cheddar Cheese, shredded
• 6 oz. Rotisserie Chicken, shredded
• 4 tablespoons Tomato Sauce
• 1 tablespoons Mayonnaise
• 4 tablespoons BBQ Sauce

INSTRUCTIONS:
1. Preheat the oven to 425 degrees Fahrenheit.
2. Blend the crust ingredients.
3. Using a silicone spatula, spread the dough out on a Silpat.
4. Bake crust for 10 minutes.
5. Flip the pizza once it's finished in the oven.
6. Add your chosen toppings and bake for another 3 minutes under the broiler.

NUTRITION:
Calories: 256 | Fat: 15 g | Carbohydrates: 75 g | Protein: 18 g | Sodium: 274 mg

Cocoa Peanut Butter Bombs

SERVINGS: 4
COOKING TIME: 20 MINUTES
DIFFICULTY: MODERATE

INGREDIENTS:
- 2 tablespoons PB Fit Powder
- ¼ cup Cocoa Powder
- 2 tablespoons Shelled Hemp Seeds
- 28 drops of Liquid Stevia
- 2 tablespoons Heavy Cream
- 1 teaspoon Vanilla Extract
- 1/2 cup Coconut Oil
- 1/4 cup Unsweetened Shredded Coconut

INSTRUCTIONS:
1. Mix the dry ingredients with the coconut oil.
2. Combine the heavy cream, vanilla, and liquid stevia in a mixing bowl. Remix until everything is well incorporated and the texture is somewhat creamy.
3. On a plate, pour unsweetened shredded coconut
4. Roll the balls in your palm, then roll in coconut.
5. Place on a lined baking tray and freeze for 20 minutes.

NUTRITION:
Calories: 207 | Fat: 18 g | Carbohydrates: 38 g | Protein: 4 g | Sodium: 205 mg

DASH Diet Edamame Tofu Bowl

SERVINGS: 4
COOKING TIME: 40 MINUTES
DIFFICULTY: MODERATE

INGREDIENTS:
• 1 yellow onion, minced
• 4 shiitake mushroom caps, sliced
• 10 ounces firm tofu, crumbled
• 1 tablespoon toasted sesame oil
• 1 teaspoon grated fresh ginger
• 1 cup shelled edamame, cooked in salted water until soft
• 2 green onions, minced
• 1 tablespoon toasted sesame seeds
• 2 tablespoons soy sauce
• 3 cups brown rice, cooked
• 1 tablespoon canola oil

INSTRUCTIONS:
1. Heat the canola oil in a skillet; Sauté the onion, about 5 minutes.
2. Add mushrooms and cook for another 5 minutes.
3. Add the ginger and green onions.
4. Add tofu and soy sauce and combine thoroughly for about 5 minutes.
5. Add the edamame and cook, stirring frequently.
6. Distribute the hot rice among four bowls, then top with the edamame and tofu combination and sesame oil.
7. Serve garnished with sesame seeds.

NUTRITION:
Calories: 107 | Fat: 2 g | Carbohydrates: 21 g | Fiber: 14 g | Protein: 5 g | Sodium: 136 mg

Tortilla Chips

SERVINGS: 4
COOKING TIME: 15 MINUTES
DIFFICULTY: EASY

INGREDIENTS:
TORTILLA CHIPS
• Flaxseed Tortillas
• Oil for Deep Frying
• Salt and Pepper to Taste
TOPPINGS
• Fresh Salsa
• Full-Fat Sour Cream
• Diced Jalapeño
• Shredded Cheese

INSTRUCTIONS:
1. Preheat the deep fryer to 350° F.
2. Fry tortilla for 2 minutes per side.
3. Remove from the fryer and set aside to cool on paper towels.
4. Season well and serve with toppings.

NUTRITION:
Calories: 165 | Fat: 8 g | Sodium: 456 mg | Carbohydrates: 43 g |
Fiber: 6 g | Sugars: 1 g | Protein: 5 g

SERVINGS: 2
COOKING TIME: 10 MINUTES
DIFFICULTY: EASY

INGREDIENTS:
- ¼ teaspoon Onion Powder
- ½ teaspoon Dried Parsley
- 3 oz. Cream Cheese
- 3 slices Bacon, cooked crisp
- ¼ teaspoon Garlic Powder
- 1 Jalapeño Pepper, sliced
- Salt and Pepper to Taste

INSTRUCTIONS:
1. Mix the cream cheese, jalapeño, spices, salt and pepper.
2. Mix in the bacon grease until it forms a firm consistency.
3. Place crumbled bacon on a platter.
4. Form into balls, then roll the balls in bacon.

NUTRITION:
Calories: 197 | Fat: 8 g | Carbohydrates: 25 g | Protein: 8 g |
Sodium: 395 mg

Low-Carb Pan Pizza Dip

SERVINGS: 2
COOKING TIME: 30 MINUTES
DIFFICULTY: MODERATE

INGREDIENTS:
• 6 oz. Cream Cheese microwaved
• ¼ cup Sour Cream
• ½ cup Mozzarella Cheese, shredded
• Salt and Pepper to Taste
• ¼ cup Mayonnaise
• ½ cup Mozzarella Cheese, shredded
• ½ cup Low-Carb Tomato Sauce
• ¼ cup Parmesan Cheese

INSTRUCTIONS:
1. Preheat the oven to 350 degrees Fahrenheit.
2. Mix the cream cheese, sour cream, mayonnaise, mozzarella, salt and pepper.
3. Pour into ramekins and spread Tomato Sauce over each ramekin as well as mozzarella cheese and parmesan cheese.
4. Top your pan pizza dips with your favorite toppings.
5. Bake for 20 minutes.
6. Serve alongside some tasty breadsticks or pork rinds!

NUTRITION:
Calories: 249 | Fat: 12 g | Carbohydrates: 29 g | Protein: 14 g | Sodium: 478 mg

Corndog Muffins

SERVINGS: 4
COOKING TIME: 25 MINUTES
DIFFICULTY: MODERATE

INGREDIENTS:
- 3 tablespoons Swerve Sweetener
- ½ cup Blanched Almond Flour
- ½ cup Flaxseed Meal
- 10 Smokies, halved
- ¼ teaspoon Low-Sodium Salt
- 1 tablespoon Psyllium Husk Powder
- ¼ cup butter, melted
- 1 Egg
- ¾ cup Sour Cream
- ¼ teaspoon Baking Powder
- ¼ cup Coconut Milk

INSTRUCTIONS:
1. Preheat the oven to 375 degrees Fahrenheit.
2. Mix all of the dry ingredients.
3. Mix in the egg, sour cream, and butter until thoroughly combined.
4. Mix in the coconut milk.
5. Place smokies in the center of the batter.
6. Bake for 12 minutes, then broil for 2 minutes.
7. Allow the muffins to cool in the tray for a few minutes before removing them to cool on a wire rack.
8. Serve with spring onion as a garnish.

NUTRITION:
Calories: 126 | Fat: 7 g | Carbohydrates: 12 g | Protein: 4 g | Sodium: 347 mg

DASH Diet Fried Queso Blanco

SERVINGS: 1
COOKING TIME: 25 MINUTES
DIFFICULTY: EASY

INGREDIENTS:
• 6 oz. Queso Blanco, cubed
• 1½ tablespoons Olive Oil
• 2 oz. Olives
• 1 pinch Red Pepper Flakes

INSTRUCTIONS:
1. Heat the oil and melt the cheese cubes.
2. Continue to heat the cheese, then fold half of it in on itself.
3. Continue to flip the cheese and heat it until a beautiful crust form.
4. Form a block with the melted cheese and seal all of the corners with another spatula, fork, or knife.
5. Remove the pan from the heat.
6. Cut into cubes and serve with olive oil and a sprinkle of pepper flakes.

NUTRITION:
Calories: 170 | Fat: 6 g | Carbohydrates: 29 g | Protein: 7 g | Sodium: 189 mg

Cheddar and Bell Pepper Pizza

SERVINGS: 2
COOKING TIME: 30 MINUTES
DIFFICULTY: EASY

INGREDIENTS:
• Pizza dough
• 4 oz. Shredded Cheddar Cheese
• 1 Vine Tomato
• ¼ cup Tomato Sauce
• ¾ Bell Pepper
• 2-3 tablespoons Fresh Basil

INSTRUCTIONS:
1. Preheat the oven to 350° F.
2. Bake the dough for about 8 minutes.
3. Slice vine tomato and place on each pizza dough, along with 2 tablespoons tomato sauce.
4. Top with shredded Cheddar cheese and bell peppers and bake another 10 minutes.
5. Serve garnished with fresh basil.

NUTRITION:
Calories: 253 | Fat: 7 g | Carbohydrates: 58 g | Protein: 6 g | Sodium: 483 mg

DASH Diet Low-Sugar Flat-Bread Pizza

SERVINGS: 2
COOKING TIME: 40 MINUTES
DIFFICULTY: MODERATE

INGREDIENTS:
PEANUT SAUCE
• 4 tablespoons PBFit
• 2 tablespoons Rice Wine Vinegar
• 4 tablespoons Coconut Oil
• 4 tablespoons Reduced Sugar Ketchup
• 1 teaspoon Fish Sauce
• 4 tablespoons Soy Sauce
• Juice of ½ Lime
• Pizza Base
TOPPINGS
• 2 Chicken Thighs, cooked
• 3 oz. Mung Bean Sprouts
• 6 oz. Mozzarella Cheese
• 2 Green Onions
• 1 ½ oz. Shredded Carrot
• 2 tablespoons Peanuts, chopped
• 3 tablespoons Cilantro, chopped

INSTRUCTIONS:
1. Preheat the oven to 400 degrees Fahrenheit.
2. Blend the sauce ingredients.
3. Mix the egg into the cheese thoroughly. Then, completely combine the dry ingredients with the cheese.
4. Place the pizza base on a Silpat and press it from edge to edge to make a huge rectangle.
5. Bake for 14 minutes until browned.
6. Set aside the pre-cooked chicken, which has been chopped into

bite-size parts.

7. Turn the pizza over and top with sauce, chicken, shredded carrots, and mozzarella; bake for another 8 minutes.

8. Garnish with mung bean sprouts, sliced spring onion, chopped peanuts, and cilantro.

NUTRITION:
Calories: 238 | Fat: 12 g | Carbohydrates: 42 g | Protein: 9 g | Sodium: 324 mg

Ham and Cheese Stromboli

SERVINGS: 4
COOKING TIME: 30 MINUTES
DIFFICULTY: EXPERT

INGREDIENTS:
• 4 tablespoons Almond Flour
• 3 tablespoons Coconut Flour
• 2 cups Mozzarella Cheese, shredded
• 1 Egg
• 5 oz. Cheddar Cheese
• 4 oz. Ham
• 1 teaspoon Italian Seasoning
• Salt and Pepper to Taste

INSTRUCTIONS:
1. Mix almond, coconut flour, and seasonings.
2. Start incorporating the melted mozzarella into your flour mixture.
3. Add your egg and stir everything together.
4. Transfer dough to a parchment paper and place another parchment paper on top; flatten it out with a rolling pin.
5. Cut diagonal lines from the edges of the dough to the center with a pizza cutter.
6. Alternate between ham and cheddar on the uncut dough stretch.
7. Then, one slice of dough at a time, lift it and place it on top of the filling, covering it completely.
8. Bake for 20 minutes.

NUTRITION:
Calories: 190 | Fat: 11 g | Carbohydrates: 32 g | Protein: 15 g | Sodium: 342 mg

Mini Portobello Pizza

SERVINGS: 4
COOKING TIME: 25 MINUTES
DIFFICULTY: EASY

INGREDIENTS:
- 1 Vine Tomato, sliced thin
- ¼ Cup Fresh Chopped Basil
- 1 pinch Low-Sodium Salt and Pepper
- 4 oz. Mozzarella Cheese
- 20 slices Pepperoni
- 6 tablespoons Olive Oil
- 4 Portobello Mushroom Caps

INSTRUCTIONS:
1. Scrape out all of the mushroom's insides.
2. Preheat the oven to high broil and brush the insides of the mushrooms with Olive Oil. Season with salt and pepper.
3. Broil the mushroom for 3 minutes.
4. Turn the mushrooms over and brush with Olive Oil, and season with salt and pepper.
5. Broil a further 4 minutes.
6. In each mushroom, place a tomato and basil leaf.
7. Top each mushroom with 5 pieces of pepperoni and fresh cubed mozzarella cheese.
8. Broil for another 2 minutes.

NUTRITION:
Calories: 180 | Fat: 9 g | Carbohydrates: 38 g | Protein: 5 g | Sodium: 463 mg

Tofu and Capers Pizza

SERVINGS: 4
COOKING TIME: 40 MINUTES
DIFFICULTY: MODERATE

INGREDIENTS:
- 2 tablespoons olive oil
- 16-ounce package of tofu, drained and sliced
- 1 pinch Low-Sodium Salt
- 3 garlic cloves, minced
- 14.5-ounce can of diced tomatoes, drained
- ¼ cup sun-dried tomatoes, sliced
- 1 tablespoon capers
- 1 teaspoon dried oregano
- ½ teaspoon sugar
- Freshly ground black pepper
- 2 tablespoons minced fresh parsley

INSTRUCTIONS:
1. Preheat the oven to 275 degrees Fahrenheit.
2. Cook tofu in an oiled skillet until the tofu is browned.
3. Season with salt and pepper.
4. Heat the remaining oil and sauté garlic for 1 minute.
5. Add all tomatoes, olives, and capers.
6. Toss in the oregano, sugar, and salt, then season to taste with pepper.
7. Cook for around ten minutes.
8. Drizzle the sauce over the fried tofu slices and garnish with parsley. Serve right away.

NUTRITION:
Calories: 185 | Fat: 8 g | Sodium: 483 mg | Carbohydrates: 73 g | Protein: 12 g

Cheesy Ramen Pizza

SERVINGS: 4
COOKING TIME: 40 MINUTES
DIFFICULTY: HARD

INGREDIENTS:
• 6 oz. ramen noodles, cooked
• 2 cups mozzarella cheese, grated
OTHER TOPPINGS
• ½ cup milk
• 4 black olives
• 1 egg, beaten
• 1 cup mushroom
• 1 can jalapeño slices
• 1 cup barbecue sauce
• ¼ cup Parmesan cheese, grated
• 1 cup bell pepper
• 1 cup cooked chicken, chopped
• 1 teaspoon red pepper flakes
• ½ red onion, sliced thinly
• 11-ounce mandarin oranges drained well

INSTRUCTIONS:
1. Preheat your oven to 350 degrees F.
2. Whisk together the egg, milk, and Parmesan cheese in a pan.
3. Stir in the noodles.
4. Cook for about 12 minutes in the oven.
5. Sprinkle the barbecue sauce over the noodles, then add the chicken, onions, and oranges.
6. Evenly sprinkle the mozzarella cheese on top.
7. Cook for around 15 minutes in the oven.

NUTRITION:

Calories: 277 | Fat: 12 g | Sodium: 578 mg | Carbohydrates: 58 g | Protein: 16 g

Pizza Breadsticks

SERVINGS: 4
COOKING TIME: 35 MINUTES
DIFFICULTY: EASY

INGREDIENTS:
BREADSTICK BASE
- 2 cups Mozzarella Cheese, melted
- ¾ cup Almond Flour
- 1 tablespoon Psyllium Husk Powder
- 3 tablespoons Cream Cheese
- 1 Egg
- 1 teaspoon Baking Powder
- 2 tablespoons Italian Seasoning
- 1 teaspoon Low-Sodium Salt
- 1 teaspoon Pepper
EXTRA TOPPINGS
- 1 teaspoon Garlic Powder
- 3 oz. Cheddar Cheese
- 1 teaspoon Onion Powder
- 1/4 cup Parmesan Cheese

INSTRUCTIONS:
1. Preheat the oven to 400 degrees Fahrenheit.
2. Whisk egg and cream cheese.
3. Mix dry ingredients in another bowl.
4. Mix the wet and dry ingredients along with the mozzarella cheese.
5. Knead the dough together with your hands. Set it on a Silpat.
6. Transfer the dough to foil so you can cut it with a pizza cutter.
7. Cut the dough into pieces and season it with salt and pepper.
8. Bake until crisp, for 14 minutes.

NUTRITION:

Calories: 232 | Fat 11 g | Carbohydrates: 67 g | Protein: 18 g | Sodium: 327 mg

Easy Peasy Pizza

SERVINGS: 2
COOKING TIME: 30 MINUTES
DIFFICULTY: EASY

INGREDIENTS:
PIZZA CRUST
• 1 tablespoon Psyllium Husk Powder
• 2 Eggs
• 2 tablespoons Parmesan Cheese
• ½ teaspoon Italian Seasoning
• Salt to Taste
• 2 teaspoon Frying Oil
TOPPINGS
• 5 oz. Mozzarella Cheese
• 3 tablespoons Low-Carb Tomato Sauce
• 1 tablespoon Freshly Chopped
• Basil

INSTRUCTIONS:
1. Preheat the broiler to high.
2. Mix all the dry ingredients.
3. Using your immersion blender, combine 2 eggs with the rest of the ingredients.
4. Heat 2 teaspoons of frying oil.
5. Spread out dough into the pan.
6. Flip once the edges look golden.
7. Cook for 50 seconds on the other side.
8. Brush low-carb tomato sauce over the pizza.
9. Top with cheese and broil for a few minutes.

NUTRITION:
Calories: 259 | Fat: 12 g | Carbohydrates: 45 g | Protein: 17 g |

Sodium: 329 mg

Sweet Potato Chicken Dumplings

SERVINGS: 4
COOKING TIME: 40 MINUTES
DIFFICULTY: EXPERT

INGREDIENTS:
- 1 cup frozen peas
- ½ cup all-purpose flour, divided
- 3 cups cooked chicken breast, shredded
- 1 cup carrots, sliced
- 2 cloves garlic, minced
- 1 teaspoon baking soda
- 2 cups low-sodium chicken broth
- 1 teaspoon black pepper, divided
- 1 cup kale, stemmed and chopped
- 1 cup wheat flour
- 1 onion, chopped
- 1 tablespoon olive oil
- 1 cup buttermilk
- 1 cup green beans, halved
- 1 sweet potato, cooked, peeled, and mashed
- ⅛ teaspoon low-sodium salt

INSTRUCTIONS:
1. In a skillet, heat the oil.
2. Sauté onions with carrots, green beans, peas, kale, garlic, and pepper for 8 minutes.
3. Cook for another 3 minutes after adding the flour.
4. Mix in the broth and bring to a boil.
5. Toss the vegetables and shredded chicken together. Evenly distribute the batter among the 16 muffin cups.
6. Combine the flours, baking soda, salt, and remaining pepper in a mixing basin.

7. Mix in the mashed sweet potato and buttermilk.

8. Transfer to muffin cups, then top with the chicken mixture.

9. Bake for 15 minutes until golden.

NUTRITION:

Calories: 188 | Fat: 9 g | Sodium: 185 mg | Carbohydrates: 29 g | Fiber: 5 g | Sugars: 3 g | Protein: 14 g

SERVINGS: 4
COOKING TIME: 20 MINUTES
DIFFICULTY: EASY

INGREDIENTS:
• 3 apples, peeled, cored, and sliced
• 1 tablespoon grated fresh ginger
• 1 teaspoon ground cinnamon
• 3 oz. Stevia powder
• 1 pinch of sea salt
• 2 tablespoons almond oil

INSTRUCTIONS:
1. In a non-stick skillet, heat the almond oil until simmering.
2. Add the ginger, apples, cinnamon, stevia, and salt.
3. Cook for 8 minutes.

NUTRITION:
Calories: 125 | Fat: 4 g | Carbohydrates: 27 g | Sugars: 4 g | Fiber: 8 g | Protein: 3 g | Sodium: 165 mg

Olive Pizza Bombs

SERVINGS: 2
COOKING TIME: 10 MINUTES
DIFFICULTY: EASY

INGREDIENTS:
• 4 oz. Cream Cheese
• 4 slices Pepperoni, diced
• 4 pitted Black Olives, diced
• 2 tablespoons Sun-Dried Tomato Pesto

INSTRUCTIONS:
1. Combine basil, tomato pesto, and cream cheese in a mixing bowl.
2. Mix in the olives and pepperoni.
3. Form into balls and garnish with pepperoni, basil, and olives.

NUTRITION:
Calories: 130 | Fat: 5 g | Carbohydrates: 37 g | Protein: 5 g |
Sodium: 225 mg

FISH & SEAFOOD RECIPES

FISH & SEAFOOD RECIPES

Shrimp Mexicana

SERVINGS: 4
COOKING TIME: 30 MINUTES
DIFFICULTY: MODERATE

INGREDIENTS:
- 1 tablespoon extra virgin olive oil
- 1 teaspoon chili powder
- 1 teaspoon low sodium salt
- 1 lb. medium shrimp, peeled and deveined
- 1 avocado, pitted and diced
- Shredded lettuce, for serving
- Fresh cilantro, for serving
- 1 lime, cut into wedges
FOR THE TORTILLAS
- 6 egg whites
- ¼ cup coconut flour
- ¼ cup almond milk
- ½ teaspoon low sodium salt
- ½ teaspoon cumin
- ¼ teaspoon chili powder

INSTRUCTIONS:
1. Combine all of the tortilla ingredient.
2. Heat a skillet and mix the olive oil, chili powder, and low sodium salt and toss with the shrimp to coat. Set aside.
3. Coat the pan with almond oil spray and pour some batter onto the skillet in a thin layer.
4. Cook for 2 minutes, flip over and cook for another 2 minutes until lightly browned.
5. Top each tortilla with shrimp, lettuce, avocado, and cilantro.

NUTRITION:

Calories: 135 | Fat: 6 g | Carbohydrates: 28 g | Fiber: 3 g | Sugars: 2 g | Protein: 14 g | Sodium: 285 mg

Lemon and Thyme Salmon

SERVINGS: 4
COOKING TIME: 40 MINUTES
DIFFICULTY: EASY

INGREDIENTS:
- 1 lemon, sliced thin
- 1 tablespoon fresh thyme
- 32 oz piece of salmon
- 1 tablespoons caper
- 1 pinch low sodium salt and freshly ground pepper
- Olive oil

INSTRUCTIONS:
1. Line a rimmed baking sheet with parchment paper.
2. Layer salmon, skin side down, on the prepared baking sheet.
3. Season with salt and pepper.
4. Arrange capers, sliced lemon and thyme on the salmon.
5. Bake at 400 degrees F for 25 minutes.

NUTRITION:
Calories: 180 | Fat: 5 g | Sodium: 284 mg | Carbohydrates: 23 g |
Fiber: 7 g | Protein: 16 g

Spinach, Shrimp & Tangerine Bowl

SERVINGS: 4
COOKING TIME: 25 MINUTES
DIFFICULTY: EASY

INGREDIENTS:
- 1 cup endive
- 1 tablespoon parsley, chopped
- ¼ small red onions, sliced in rings
- 3 cups spinach
- 1 tablespoon clarified butter
- ½ cup cooked shrimp (tails removed)
- 2 small tangerines, peeled and sectioned
- ¼ cup roasted pine nuts
- 1 tablespoon basil, chopped
- 1 teaspoon fresh lime juice

INSTRUCTIONS:
1. Combine the onion, spinach, endive, basil, and parsley in a large salad bowl.
2. Heat butter and cook the shrimp and lime together for one minute.
3. Toss the shrimp, pine nuts, and dressing of your choice into the salad bowl mix to combine.
4. Serve the salad with tangerine wedges as a garnish.

NUTRITION:
Calories: 138 | Fat: 5 g | Sodium: 220 mg | Carbohydrates: 16 g | Fiber: 19 g | Protein: 15 g

Black Pepper Salmon with Yogurt

SERVINGS: 4
COOKING TIME: 25 MINUTES
DIFFICULTY: EASY

INGREDIENTS:
YOGURT MARINADE
• ¼ teaspoon cayenne powder
• ¼ cup low-fat Greek yogurt
• ½ teaspoon coriander powder
• ½ teaspoon ginger powder
• ½ teaspoon turmeric powder
• 1 pinch Low-Sodium Salt
• 1 pinch ground black pepper
SALMON
• 4 skinless salmon fillets

INSTRUCTIONS:
1. Heat the broiler.
2. Place the salmon fillets in a single layer on the broiler pan.
3. Spoon the yogurt mixture evenly over each fillet.
4. Grill for about 15 minutes.

NUTRITION:
Calories: 172 | Fat: 5 g | Carbohydrates: 24 g | Fiber: 6 g | Sugars: 2 g | Protein: 19 g | Sodium: 243 mg

Cod in Tomato Sauce

SERVINGS: 5
COOKING TIME: 50 MINUTES
DIFFICULTY: MODERATE

INGREDIENTS:
- 2 tablespoons olive oil
- 3 tablespoons of tomato paste
- 1 teaspoon dried dill weed
- 2 teaspoons sumac
- 2 teaspoons ground coriander
- 1½ teaspoons ground cumin
- 1 teaspoon turmeric powder
- 1 sweet onion, diced
- 8 garlic cloves, crushed
- 2 jalapeño peppers, chopped
- 2 tablespoons lime juice
- 5 medium tomatoes, chopped
- ½ cup of water
- 5 cod fillets
- 1 pinch low-sodium salt
- 1 pinch ground black pepper

INSTRUCTIONS:
1. For the spice mix: Place the dill and spices in a bowl and mix well.
2. Heat the oil in a wok and sauté the onion for about 2 minutes.
3. Sauté for around 2 minutes with the garlic and jalapeño.
4. Stir in the tomatoes, tomato paste, lime juice, water, half the spice blend, salt, and pepper, and bring to a boil.
5. Cook, covered, for about 10 minutes over medium-low heat, stirring periodically.
6. Season the cod fillets evenly with the remaining spice blend, salt, and pepper.

7. Place the fish fillets in the wok and press lightly into the tomato mixture.
8. Set the heat to medium-high and cook for about 2 minutes.
9. Simmer, covered, for about 15 minutes.

NUTRITION:
Calories: 183 | Fat: 6 g | Carbohydrates: 34 g | Fiber: 5 g | Sugars: 3 g | Protein: 14 g | Sodium: 285 mg

DASH Diet-Friendly Ginger Tilapia

SERVINGS: 5
COOKING TIME: 20 MINUTES
DIFFICULTY: EASY

INGREDIENTS:
- 5 tilapia fillets
- 3 garlic cloves, crushed
- 2 tablespoons fresh ginger, chopped
- 2 tablespoons unsweetened coconut, grated
- 2 tablespoons coconut aminos
- 8 spring onions, chopped
- 2 tablespoons almond oil

INSTRUCTIONS:
1. In a skillet, melt the almond oil over high heat and fry the tilapia fillets for about 2 minutes per side.
2. Add the garlic, coconut, and ginger and cook for 1 minute.
3. Add the coconut aminos and cook for another 1 minute.
4. Add the spring onion and cook for about 2 minutes more.

NUTRITION:
Calories: 166 | Fat: 7 g | Carbohydrates: 24 g | Fiber: 3 g | Sugars: 1.5 g | Protein: 12 g | Sodium: 180 mg

Swiss Chard & Haddock

SERVINGS: 1
COOKING TIME: 25 MINUTES
DIFFICULTY: EASY

INGREDIENTS:
• 2 tablespoons almond oil
• 2 garlic cloves, crushed
• 2 teaspoons fresh ginger, finely grated
• 1 fillet of haddock
• Salt and ground black pepper
• 2 cups Swiss chard, coarsely chopped
• 1 teaspoon coconut aminos

INSTRUCTIONS:
1. In a saucepan, melt and sweat 1 tablespoon of almond oil over medium heat
2. For about 1 minute, sauté the garlic and ginger.
3. Add the haddock along with salt and pepper; cook for 4 minutes on each side.
4. In another pan, melt remaining almond oil and cook the chard and coconut aminos for about 8 minutes.
5. Serve the salmon fillet on the chard.

NUTRITION:
Calories: 112 | Fat: 3 g | Carbohydrates: 20 g | Fiber: 5 g | Sugars: 1.4 g | Protein: 16 g | Sodium: 192 mg

Lemon Prawns

SERVINGS: 4
COOKING TIME: 25 MINUTES
DIFFICULTY: MODERATE

INGREDIENTS:
- 1 onion, diced
- 1 tablespoon fresh ginger, chopped
- 3 garlic cloves, crushed
- 1 tablespoon fresh lemon zest, finely grated
- 1 fresh red pepper, seeded and chopped
- 1 teaspoon ground turmeric
- ½ cup olive oil
- ½ cup fresh lemon juice
- 20-24 raw shrimp, peeled and deveined
- 1 tablespoon almond oil

INSTRUCTIONS:
1. In a bowl, combine all ingredients except shrimp and almond oil.
2. Add shrimp and brush generously with marinade.
3. Cover and marinate in the fridge overnight.
4. Melt the almond oil in a non-stick skillet over high heat and sauté shrimp for 3 minutes.
5. Add the reserved marinade and bring to a boil, stirring occasionally.
6. Cook for about 1-2 minutes.

NUTRITION:
Calories: 168 | Fat: 7 g | Carbohydrates: 25 g | Fiber: 4 g | Sugars: 1 g | Protein: 12 g | Sodium: 185 mg

Prawns with Asparagus

SERVINGS: 4
COOKING TIME: 25 MINUTES
DIFFICULTY: EASY

INGREDIENTS:
• 1 bunch of asparagus, peeled and chopped
• 1-pound shrimp, peeled and deveined
• ¾ cup chicken broth
• 4 garlic cloves, crushed
• ½ teaspoon ground ginger
• 2 tablespoons fresh lemon juice
• 2 tablespoons almond oil

INSTRUCTIONS:
1. In a skillet over medium heat, melt the almond oil.
2. Add everything (except broth) and cook for about 2 minutes.
3. Stir and cook for about 5 minutes.
4. Add broth and cook for about 2 to 4 minutes.

NUTRITION:
Calories: 155 | Fat: 6 g | Carbohydrates: 18 g | Fiber: 12 g | Protein: 20 g | Sodium: 190 mg

DASH Diet-Friendly Shrimp Curry

SERVINGS: 4
COOKING TIME: 35 MINUTES
DIFFICULTY: MODERATE

INGREDIENTS:
- ½ sweet onion, diced
- 2 garlic cloves, crushed
- 1½ teaspoons ground turmeric
- 1 teaspoon cumin powder
- 1 teaspoon paprika
- ½ teaspoon red chili powder
- 1 teaspoon ginger powder
- 14-ounces can of coconut milk
- 2 tablespoons olive oil
- 14½-ounces diced low-sodium tomatoes
- 1 pinch of salt
- 1 pound cooked shrimp, peeled and deveined
- 2 tablespoons fresh cilantro, chopped

INSTRUCTIONS:
1. In a skillet, heat the oil and sauté the onion for about 5 minutes.
2. Sauté for 1 minute after adding the garlic and seasonings.
3. Add the coconut milk, tomatoes, and salt and simmer for about 10 minutes.
4. Stir in the prawns and cilantro and simmer for about 2 minutes.

NUTRITION:
Calories: 188 | Fat: 9 g | Carbohydrates: 17 g | Fiber: 6 g | Sugars: 1.7 g | Protein: 18 g | Sodium: 170 mg

Fruit Prawn Curry

SERVINGS: 4
COOKING TIME: 30 MINUTES
DIFFICULTY: EASY

INGREDIENTS:
• 2 teaspoons almond oil
• ½ cup onion, thinly sliced
• 1½ pounds peeled and deveined shrimp
• ½ red bell pepper, seeded and sliced
• 1 mango, peeled, pitted, and sliced
• 8-ounce of pineapple chunks
• 1 cup coconut milk
• 1 Tablespoon red curry paste
• 2 tablespoons of fish sauce
• 2 tablespoons fresh cilantro, chopped

INSTRUCTIONS:
1. In a skillet, melt a teaspoon of almond oil and sauté the onion for 4 minutes.
2. Push the onion to the edge of the pan.
3. Add the remaining oil and the shrimp; sauté 2 minutes on each side.
4. Cook for 3 minutes after adding the paprika.
5. Add the rest of the ingredients, and cook for 5 minutes.
6. Garnish with cilantro and serve.

NUTRITION:
Calories: 110 | Fat: 3 g | Carbohydrates: 19 g | Fiber: 6 g | Sugars: 4 g | Protein: 10 g | Sodium: 188 mg

Shrimp and Scallop Combo

SERVINGS: 4
COOKING TIME: 45 MINUTES
DIFFICULTY: MODERATE

INGREDIENTS:
- ½ cup chopped scallions
- 4 tablespoons clarified butter, divided
- 1 clove of garlic, minced or pressed
- ½ cup green bell peppers, seeded and diced
- ½ cup vegetable broth
- 1-pound jumbo raw shrimp, peeled and de-veined
- 1-pound bay scallops
- 3 tablespoons chopped basil
- 2 tablespoons chopped parsley
- 1 teaspoon marjoram
- 1 cup broccoli florets, steamed in the microwave
- ½ cup soy milk
- 2 tablespoons spelt flour
- 2 cups diced tomatoes
- 12 ounces cooked spelt or vegetable pasta

INSTRUCTIONS:
1. Melt 2 tablespoons of butter and sauté the garlic, onions, and bell peppers for 5 minutes.
2. Add the vegetable broth and cook until the broth has evaporated.
3. Drain pasta and set aside according to package guidelines.
4. Bring soy milk to a low boil in a pot.
5. Add in the spelt flour, until the mixture thickens.
6. Melt the remaining butter in a pan over medium heat.
7. Combine the shrimp, scallops, basil, parsley, and marjoram in a mixing bowl. Gently swirl and simmer for 3 minutes, uncovered until the seafood is done.

8. Toss all ingredients with cooked pasta and serve immediately.

NUTRITION:
Calories: 176 | Fat: 5 g | Sodium: 232 mg | Carbohydrate: 27 g |
Fiber: 11 g | Protein: 18 g

Orange Poached Salmon

SERVINGS: 3
COOKING TIME: 30 MINUTES
DIFFICULTY: EASY

INGREDIENTS:
• 1 teaspoon ginger, minced
• ½ cup fresh orange juice
• 3 tablespoons coconut aminos
• 4 garlic cloves, crushed
• 3 salmon fillets

INSTRUCTIONS:
1. Mix all the ingredients except the salmon.
2. Layer salmon fillets in a skillet and spread the ginger mixture over the salmon; bring to a boil.
3. Simmer, covered, for 9 minutes.

NUTRITION:
Calories: 189 | Fat: 8 g | Carbohydrates: 23 g | Fiber: 6 g | Protein: 21 g | Sodium: 250 mg

Paprika Salmon

SERVINGS: 6
COOKING TIME: 20 MINUTES
DIFFICULTY: EASY

INGREDIENTS:
• ½ tablespoon ground ginger
• ½ tablespoon ground coriander
• ½ tablespoon ground cumin
• ½ teaspoon paprika
• ¼ teaspoon cayenne pepper
• 1 pinch of salt
• 1 tablespoon of fresh orange juice
• 1 tablespoon coconut oil, melted
• 6 salmon fillets

INSTRUCTIONS:
1. Preheat the gas grill and coat the grill grate with oil.
2. Place all ingredients except salmon in a bowl and stir until paste forms.
3. Add the salmon and brush generously with the mixture.
4. Allow 30 minutes in the refrigerator to marinate.
5. Grill salmon for about 4 minutes on each side.

NUTRITION:
Calories: 185 | Fat: 6 g | Carbohydrates: 14 g | Fiber: 3 g | Sugars: 1.3 g | Protein: 17 g | Sodium: 355 mg

Honey & Amino Glazed Salmon

SERVINGS: 6
COOKING TIME: 30 MINUTES
DIFFICULTY: EASY

INGREDIENTS:
- 1 shallot, chopped
- 1 teaspoon garlic powder
- ¼ cup raw honey
- ½ cup fresh orange juice
- ½ cup coconut aminos
- 6 salmon fillets
- 1 teaspoon ginger powder

INSTRUCTIONS:
1. Put all the ingredients in a Ziploc bag and seal the bag.
2. Shake the bag to coat the salmon mixture.
3. Preheat grill to medium heat.
4. Remove the salmon from the marinade bag and set it aside.
5. Grill for about 15 minutes.

NUTRITION:
Calories: 196 | Fat: 7 g | Carbohydrates: 16 g | Fiber: 8 g | Sugars: 1.5 g | Protein: 20 g | Sodium: 279 mg

Crusted Salmon with Dill

SERVINGS: 4
COOKING TIME: 35 MINUTES
DIFFICULTY: EASY

INGREDIENTS:
• 1 cup almonds, ground
• 1 pinch black pepper
• 1 tablespoon fresh dill, chopped
• 4 teaspoons fresh lemon juice
• 2 tablespoons fresh lemon zest, grated
• ½ teaspoons garlic salt
• 1 tablespoon olive oil
• 4 tablespoons Dijon mustard
• 4 salmon fillets

INSTRUCTIONS:
1. Pulse the dill, lemon zest, garlic salt, black pepper, and butter into a crumbly mixture.
2. Layer salmon on a rimmed baking sheet
3. Spread Dijon mustard on top of each salmon fillet.
4. Spread the nut mixture evenly over each fillet.
5. Bake for about 15 minutes.

NUTRITION:
Calories: 170 | Fat: 6 g | Carbohydrates: 18 g | Fiber: 4 g | Sodium: 260 mg | Sugars: 1 g | Protein: 15 g

Black Pepper Peach and Salmon

SERVINGS: 4
COOKING TIME: 30 MINUTES
DIFFICULTY: EASY

INGREDIENTS:
- 1 pinch low-sodium salt
- 4 salmon steaks
- 3 peaches, cored and quartered
- 1 tablespoon fresh ginger, chopped
- 1 teaspoon fresh thyme leaves, chopped
- 1 tablespoon balsamic vinegar
- 3 tablespoons of olive oil
- 1 pinch ground black pepper

INSTRUCTIONS:
1. Preheat grill to medium heat.
2. Rub salmon gently with salt and black pepper.
3. Grill peaches and salmon for 5 minutes on each side.
4. Combine the remaining ingredients and spoon over the salmon.
5. Serve with the peaches and onions.

NUTRITION:
Calories: 210 | Fat: 8 g | Carbohydrates: 21 g | Fiber: 4 g | Sodium: 384 mg | Protein: 15 g

Sea Bass with Vegetables

SERVINGS: 2
COOKING TIME: 30 MINUTES
DIFFICULTY: MODERATE

INGREDIENTS:
• 1 sea bass fillet, diced
• 1 tablespoon coconut vinegar
• ¼ teaspoon garlic pacto
• ¼ cup yellow bell peppers, seeded and diced
• 1 teaspoon red pepper powder
• 1 tablespoon olive oil, extra-virgin
• ½ cup fresh button mushrooms, sliced
• 1 small onion, quartered
• ¼ teaspoon ginger paste
• ¼ cup red bell pepper, seeded and diced
• 1 pinch of salt
• 2-3 spring onions, chopped
• 1 teaspoon fish sauce

INSTRUCTIONS:
1. Combine fish, ginger, garlic, chili powder, and salt in a bowl and let sit for about 20 minutes.
2. Heat 1 teaspoon of oil in a skillet and sear the fish for 4 minutes on all sides. Set aside.
3. Heat the remaining oil and cook the mushrooms and onions, about 6 minutes.
4. Sauté the peppers and salmon for around 2 minutes.
5. Toss in the spring onions and fish sauce and cook for about 3 minutes.

NUTRITION:
Calories: 180 | Fat: 9 g | Carbohydrates: 18 g | Fiber: 5 g | Sodium:

183 mg | Sugars: 1.8 g | Protein: 17 g

SALAD RECIPES

SALAD RECIPES

Spinach, Rocket, and Avocado Salad

SERVINGS: 3-4
COOKING TIME: 15 MINUTES
DIFFICULTY: EASY

INGREDIENTS:
- 18 tablespoon of baby spinach
- 1 onion
- ½ chopped avocado
- Juice of ½ lemon
- 1 handful rocket
- Avocado or olive oil
- Himalayan salt & black pepper

INSTRUCTIONS:
1. Wash all of the greens thoroughly and set them in a big salad dish.
2. Thinly slice the red onion, chop the avocado, and toss the leaves together. Make the avocado fairly rough so that it becomes a component of the dressing and partially coats the leaves.
3. Drizzle the salad with oil after squeezing the lemon juice over it. To taste, season with salt and pepper.

NUTRITION:
Calories: 74 | Carbohydrates: 18 g | Fiber: 15 g | Protein: 13 g | Sodium: 92 mg

Lettuce and Spinach Herb Salad

SERVINGS: 3-4
COOKING TIME: 10 MINUTES
DIFFICULTY: EASY

INGREDIENTS:
• Lambs leaf lettuce, torn
• Romaine lettuce, torn
• 1 bunch of baby spinach leaves
• Fresh coriander
• Fresh parsley
• Fennel
• 2 spring onions, sliced
• 1/2 lemon juice
• Olive oil

INSTRUCTIONS:
1. Combine all ingredients in a mixing bowl.

NUTRITION:
Calories: 73| Protein: 5 g | Carbohydrates: 11 g | Fiber: 14 g |
Sugars: 1.2 g | Fat: 1 g | Sodium: 108 mg

DASH Diet-Friendly Cabbage and Carrot Coleslaw

SERVINGS: 2
COOKING TIME: 10 MINUTES
DIFFICULTY: EASY

INGREDIENTS:
- ½ red cabbage, shredded
- ½ green cabbage, shredded
- 1 carrot, sliced thin
- 1 courgette, sliced thin
- Handful of parsley
- ½ lime
- 1 chili
- 2 tablespoons of avocado oil
- Himalayan salt

INSTRUCTIONS:
1. Combine everything in a mixing bowl.
2. Enjoy.

NUTRITION:
Calories: 62 | Carbohydrates: 9 g | Fiber: 18 g | Protein: 10 g |
Sodium: 92 mg

Mixed Fruit Salad

SERVINGS: 5
COOKING TIME: 15 MINUTES
DIFFICULTY: EASY

INGREDIENTS:
• 5 cups pineapple, peeled, cored, and chopped
• 2 mangoes, peeled, pitted, and chopped
• 2 Fuji apples, cored and chopped
• 2 red Bartlett pears, cored and chopped
• 2 teaspoons fresh ginger, finely grated
• 2 tablespoons of raw honey
• ¼ cup fresh lemon juice
• 2 oranges, peeled and sliced

INSTRUCTIONS:
1. Combine all the fruits in a bowl.
2. Combine the remaining ingredients in a mixing dish and whisk thoroughly.
3. Toss the fruit combined with the honey mixture to thoroughly coat it.

NUTRITION:
Calories: 71 | Fat: 1 g | Carbohydrates: 9 g | Fiber: 16 g | Sugars: 5 g | Protein: 3 g | Sodium: 48 mg

Roman Tuna Salad

SERVINGS: 2
COOKING TIME: 10 MINUTES
DIFFICULTY: EASY

INGREDIENTS:
• 1 tablespoon lemon juice
• 2 ribs of celery, diced finely
• 1 clove of garlic, minced
• 3 tablespoons parsley
• 2 tablespoons of extra virgin olive oil
• 10 sun-dried tomatoes, softened in warm water and chopped
• 10 oz. can of tuna, flaked
• 1 pinch low sodium salt and pepper

INSTRUCTIONS:
1. Toss everything in a mixing bowl.
2. Enjoy.

NUTRITION:
Calories: 128 | Fat: 6 g | Carbohydrates: 13 g | Protein: 21 g |
Sodium: 235 mg

Leftover Turkey Taco Salad

SERVINGS: 2
COOKING TIME: 40 MINUTES
DIFFICULTY: MODERATE

INGREDIENTS:
- 1 tablespoon coconut or olive oil
- ½ lbs. leftover turkey, cooked and chopped
- 1½ tablespoons taco seasoning
- ¼ cup water
- 1 tablespoon of rice vinegar
- Shredded lettuce

TACO SEASONING
- 1 teaspoon of red pepper flakes
- 1 teaspoon garlic powder
- 2 teaspoons of paprika
- 1 teaspoon onion powder
- 1 teaspoon oregano
- 3 tablespoons of chili powder
- 2 teaspoons cumin
- 4 teaspoons of low sodium salt

TOPPINGS
- Red Onion
- Sliced Olives
- Tomatoes
- Avocado
- Bell Peppers
- Crushed Sweet Potato Chips

INSTRUCTIONS:
1. In a skillet, heat oil and add the chicken; cook until the liquid has evaporated, stirring in the water and taco seasoning.
2. Prepare all of your toppings by shredding, chopping, and dicing

them.

3. Combine lettuce, toppings, chicken, remaining oil and vinegar dressing, and smashed chips in a salad bowl.

NUTRITION:

Calories: 152 | Fat: 6 g | Sodium: 346 mg | Carbohydrates: 23 g | Fiber: 15 g | Sugars: 2 g | Protein: 18 g

Low-Sodium Salad with Capers

SERVINGS: 2
COOKING TIME: 15 MINUTES
DIFFICULTY: EASY

INGREDIENTS:
• 5 cups of any salad greens
DRESSING
• ½ cup olive oil
• 3 tablespoons lemon juice
• 1 pinch low sodium salt and pepper
• 1 tablespoon pure mustard powder
• 3 tablespoons capers, minced

INSTRUCTIONS:
1. Combine the oil, lemon juice, and mustard in a mixing bowl.
2. Add veggies and mix thoroughly.
3. Capers, low sodium salt, and pepper should be added now.
4. Serve.

NUTRITION:
Calories: 126 | Fat: 3 g | Carbohydrates: 14 g | Sugars: 2 g |
Sodium: 97 mg | Fiber: 16 g | Protein: 7 g

Mixed Green Salad with Beets

SERVINGS: 3
COOKING TIME: 45 MINUTES
DIFFICULTY: EASY

INGREDIENTS:
• 2 teaspoon honey
• 2 tablespoons raw sunflower seeds, toasted in butter
• ½ cup reduced-fat feta cheese, crumbled
• 2 medium beets, boiled until fork-tender, peeled and diced
• ⅛ teaspoon low-sodium salt
• 1 orange, sliced
• 2 tablespoons calcium-fortified orange juice
• ⅛ teaspoon black pepper
• ¼ cup olive oil
• 3 cups packed mixed salad greens

INSTRUCTIONS:
1. Combine garlic, orange juice, honey, salt, and pepper; whisk in the olive oil.
2. Combine beets, sunflower seeds, orange segments, mixed greens, and feta cheese in a large serving bowl.
3. Drizzle with the dressing.

NUTRITION:
Calories: 130 | Fat: 4 g | Sodium: 104 mg | Carbohydrates: 9 g | Fiber: 12 g | Sugars: 1 g | Protein: 9 g

Farro Salad with Sweet Pea Pesto

SERVINGS: 4
COOKING TIME: 20 MINUTES
DIFFICULTY: EASY

INGREDIENTS:
• 2 cups cherry or grape tomatoes
• ¼ cup parmesan cheese
• 2 cups peas
• ½ cup low-sodium canned white beans
• 2 cloves garlic
• 1 teaspoon black pepper
• ¼ cup olive oil
• 2 tablespoons sunflower seeds, Hulled
• 1 cup farro, cooked and cooled
• Zest of 1 lemon
• 1 bell pepper, diced

INSTRUCTIONS:
1. Pulse peas, parmesan, garlic, sunflower seeds, and pepper until the peas are finely minced; slowly drip in the olive oil.
2. Combine everything in a mixing dish.

NUTRITION:
Calories: 124 | Fat: 2 g | Sodium: 106 mg | Carbohydrates: 18 g | Fiber: 9 g | Sugars: 1.4 g | Protein: 8 g

Cheesy Lemon Quinoa Salad

SERVINGS: 4
COOKING TIME: 15 MINUTES
DIFFICULTY: EASY

INGREDIENTS:
• Juice of ½ lemon
• 2 cloves garlic, minced
• 1 teaspoon low-sodium salt
• 2 tablespoons olive oil
• 1 small yellow bell pepper, diced
• 1 teaspoon black pepper
• 1 cucumber diced
• 1 tablespoon dill, chopped
• 1 cup reduced-fat feta cheese, crumbled
• 1 cup quinoa, cooked
• 1 cup cherry tomatoes, quartered

INSTRUCTIONS:
1. Whisk olive oil, garlic, lemon juice, salt, and pepper.
2. Toss everything with the dressing.

NUTRITION:
Calories: 85 | Fat: 2 g | Sodium: 94 mg | Carbohydrates: 13 g | Fiber: 16 g | Sugars: 1 g | Protein: 7 g

SERVINGS: 6
COOKING TIME: 15 MINUTES
DIFFICULTY: EASY

INGREDIENTS:
• 1 bell pepper, seeded, cut into ½-inch pieces
• 1 cup avocado, cubed
• 2 tablespoons lime juice
• 1 teaspoon low-sodium salt
• 2 green onions, sliced
• 15-ounce can, of low-sodium whole kernel corn
• 1 teaspoon chili powder
• 1 jalapeño pepper, diced
• 15-ounce can black beans, drained
• 2 mangos, cut into ½-inch cubes
• 2 tablespoons fresh cilantro, chopped
• 1 tablespoon olive oil
• 1 teaspoon black pepper
• Shredded lettuce

INSTRUCTIONS:
1. Divide lettuce among 6 plated.
2. Mix the black beans, corn, mango, avocado, onions, and jalapeño pepper.
3. Blend the lime juice, olive oil, cilantro, chili powder, black pepper, and salt in a jar with a secure lid and shake vigorously to combine. Pour the mango-avocado mixture on top.
4. Drizzle over lettuce and mixed greens, gently tossing to coat.

NUTRITION:
Calories: 85 | Fat: 2 g | Sodium: 88 mg | Carbohydrates: 5 g | Fiber: 19 g | Sugars: 3 g | Protein: 4 g

Arugula & Pear Salad with Walnuts

SERVINGS: 4
COOKING TIME: 20 MINUTES
DIFFICULTY: EASY

INGREDIENTS:
SALAD
• 4 cups arugula, trimmed, washed, and dried
• 2 firm red Bartlett pears, cut into 16 wedges
• ½ cup walnuts, chopped and toasted
• 5 cups butter-head lettuce
DRESSING
• 2 tablespoons minced shallot
• ½ teaspoon Dijon mustard
• 1 pinch freshly ground pepper
• 3 tablespoons extra-virgin olive oil
• 3 tablespoons vegetable broth
• 1 ½ tablespoon balsamic vinegar
• ¼ teaspoon low-sodium salt

INSTRUCTIONS:
1. Whisk the shallot, broth, oil, vinegar, mustard, salt, and pepper.
2. Half-fill a big mixing bowl with water. Toss with 1 tablespoon of the dressing to coat.
3. In a mixing bowl, combine the lettuce, arugula, and remaining dressing.
4. Top with walnuts and serve.

NUTRITION:
Calories: 95 | Fat: 2 g | Sodium: 104 mg | Carbohydrates: 14 g | Fiber: 3 g | Sugars: 5 g | Protein: 6 g

Loaded Greens and Seeds DASH-Friendly Salad

SERVINGS: 3-4
COOKING TIME: 15 MINUTES
DIFFICULTY: EASY

INGREDIENTS:
• 6 teaspoon tofu
• 1 Handful of rocket leaves
• 1 bunches of cos lettuce
• 1 Handful of lamb's lettuce
• 2 bunches of baby spinach
• ½ can of chickpeas
• 1 avocado
• 1 handful of seeds & nuts
• 6 cherry tomatoes
• ½ cucumber
• 1 serve of quinoa, cooked
• ½ green or red pepper
• Olive oil
• Lemon
• Himalayan salt & black pepper

INSTRUCTIONS:
1. Fry the tofu lightly in almond oil.
2. Toss everything together.

NUTRITION:
Calories: 90 | Carbohydrates: 15 g | Protein: 7 g | Fat: 2 g | Sodium: 68 mg

Carrot, Spinach & Almond Salad

SERVINGS: 2
COOKING TIME: 20 MINUTES
DIFFICULTY: EASY

INGREDIENTS:
- 1 bunch of baby spinach leaves
- 1 carrot
- ¼ red cabbage, shredded
- 2 spring onions, cut lengthways
- A handful of almonds, sliced
- 1 clove of garlic, minced
- ¼ grapefruit
- ½ lemon
- Olive oil

INSTRUCTIONS:
1. Toss all of the ingredients in a salad bowl.
2. Dress with lemon and olive oil.

NUTRITION:
Calories: 74 | Carbohydrates: 12 g | Fiber: 21 g | Protein: 13 g | Sodium: 49 mg

POULTRY RECIPES

POULTRY RECIPES

Chicken and Mushroom Casserole

SERVINGS: 4
COOKING TIME: 50 MINUTES
DIFFICULTY: MODERATE

INGREDIENTS:
- ½ cup Dijon mustard
- ½ cup raw honey
- 1 teaspoon basil (dried)
- 4 breasts of chicken
- ¼ teaspoon ground turmeric
- 1 cup fresh button mushrooms, sliced
- 1 teaspoon crumbled dried basil
- 1 pinch low-sodium salt
- 1 pinch black pepper, ground
- ½ head of broccoli, cut into florets

INSTRUCTIONS:
1. Preheat your oven to 350° F and oil a baking dish.
2. Mix all the ingredients except the chicken, mushrooms, and broccoli.
3. Arrange the chicken, broccoli florets and mushrooms in the oiled casserole dish.
4. Spoon half of the honey mixture evenly over the chicken and broccoli.
5. Bake for about 20 minutes.
6. Baste remaining sauce over the chicken and bake for another 10 minutes.

NUTRITION:
Calories: 206 | Fat: 11 g | Carbohydrates: 27 g | Fiber: 4 g | Sugars: 1 g | Protein: 18 g | Sodium: 385 mg

Roasted Lemon Herb Chicken

SERVINGS: 4
COOKING TIME: 90 MINUTES
DIFFICULTY: EASY

INGREDIENTS:
- 1 medium onion, sliced thin
- 12 pieces of bone-in chicken thighs & legs
- 1 teaspoon dried thyme
- 1 tablespoon dried rosemary
- 1 orange, sliced thin
- 1 lemon,

FOR THE MARINADE
- 2 drops of stevia
- 3 tablespoons extra virgin olive oil
- 1 pinch low sodium salt and freshly ground pepper
- 1 teaspoon onion powder
- Juice of 1 lemon
- 1 tablespoon Italian seasoning
- 3 cloves of garlic, minced
- Juice of 1 orange
- Dash of red pepper flakes

INSTRUCTIONS:
1. Mix all of the marinade ingredients with chicken in a baking dish.
2. Layer the onion, orange, and lemon slices on top of the chicken.
3. Season with thyme, rosemary, low sodium salt, and pepper.
4. Cover and bake for 30 minutes.
5. Uncover and bake for another 30 minutes.

NUTRITION:
Calories: 195 | Protein: 23 g | Carbohydrates: 19 g | Fiber: 4 g | Fat: 7 g | Sodium: 328 mg

Sunflower Seed Pesto Chicken

SERVINGS: 4
COOKING TIME: 30 MINUTES
DIFFICULTY: EASY

INGREDIENTS:
PESTO
• 2 tablespoons parmesan cheese, grated
• 1 clove of garlic, chopped
• 2 tablespoons raw, hulled sunflower seeds
• ¼ cup olive oil
• ⅛ teaspoon low-sodium salt
• ⅛ teaspoon black pepper
• 1 cup basil leaves
CHICKEN AND GARNISHES
• 2 boneless, skinless chicken breasts, sliced lengthwise
• ¼ cup part-skim mozzarella cheese, shredded and divided
• 2 tomatoes, sliced

INSTRUCTIONS:
1. Place the chicken on a rimmed baking sheet that has been oiled.
2. Blitz the pesto ingredients in a food processor.
3. Layer chicken with pesto, tomato slices, and mozzarella.
4. Bake for 15 minutes.

NUTRITION:
Calories: 204 | Fat: 11 g | Sodium: 345 mg | Carbohydrates: 23 g |
Fiber: 6 g | Protein: 22 g

Hearty Cauliflower Rice with Chicken

SERVINGS: 4
COOKING TIME: 30 MINUTES
DIFFICULTY: MODERATE

INGREDIENTS:
- 1 tablespoon honey
- 3 tablespoons oil
- 2 boneless, skinless chicken breasts, cubed
- 1 cup frozen peas and carrots, mixed
- 1 teaspoon turmeric powder
- 1 teaspoon fresh ginger, grated
- 3 cloves garlic, minced
- ¼ teaspoon black pepper
- 2 tablespoons rice wine vinegar
- ¾ cup orange juice
- 1 head cauliflower
- 3 scallions, sliced, whites & greens divided
- 1 tablespoon corn starch
- ½ red bell pepper, diced
- 1½ tablespoons low-sodium soy sauce
- 2 large eggs, beaten

INSTRUCTIONS:
1. Whisk orange juice, rice wine vinegar, soy sauce, honey, cornstarch, and ginger.
2. Scramble the eggs well.
3. Toss in the peas and carrots, scallion, garlic, and bell pepper with the remaining tablespoon of oil in the skillet, about 4 minutes.
4. Toss in the riced cauliflower, coated with cooking spray.
5. Cook for another 5 minutes, stirring regularly, or until cauliflower is somewhat crunchy.
6. In a skillet with the cauliflower, sauté the cooked chicken, eggs,

veggies, and sauce until the sauce thickens, about 3 minutes.
7. Serve garnished with scallion greens.

NUTRITION:
Calories: 162 | Fat: 5 g | Sodium: 275 mg | Carbohydrates: 21 g | Fiber: 11 g | Protein: 15 g

Spicy Turkey Stir Fry

SERVINGS: 3
COOKING TIME: 45 MINUTES
DIFFICULTY: MODERATE

INGREDIENTS:
- 1 teaspoon garam masala
- 2 bell peppers, thinly sliced
- 2 tablespoons coconut oil
- 1 pinch low sodium salt
- 2 teaspoons freshly ground pepper
- 2 lbs. boneless skinless turkey breasts, sliced
- 1 teaspoon cumin seeds
FOR THE MARINADE
- 1 teaspoon ginger, minced
- 1 clove of garlic, minced
- ½ cup coconut cream
- ¼ teaspoon turmeric
- 1 teaspoon low sodium salt

INSTRUCTIONS:
1. Combine the marinade ingredients with the chicken and set aside for 1 hour.
2. In a wok or large sauté pan, melt the coconut oil over medium-high heat, then add the cumin seeds and cook for 3 minutes.
3. After adding the marinated chicken, cook for 5 minutes and then stir in the peppers, garam masala, and pepper.
4. Add a pinch of low-sodium salt to taste.
5. Cook for 5 minutes, stirring regularly.

NUTRITION:
Calories: 183 | Fat: 6 g | Sodium: 426 mg | Carbohydrates: 23 g | Fiber: 11 g | Protein: 14 g

Roasted Balsamic Chicken

SERVINGS: 4
COOKING TIME: 270 MINUTES
DIFFICULTY: HARD

INGREDIENTS:
• Black pepper, freshly ground
• 1 chicken (whole) chopped into pieces
• 2 tablespoons mustard (Dijon)
• 1 tablespoon balsamic vinegar
• 2 tablespoons freshly squeezed lemon juice
• Chicken broth
• 1 tablespoon minced fresh parsley leaves
• 1 teaspoon lemon zest
• 2 minced garlic cloves
• 2 tablespoons olive oil
• ½ tablespoon salt

INSTRUCTIONS:
1. Preheat the oven to 400 degrees Fahrenheit.
2. Whisk the vinegar, mustard, lemon juice, garlic, olive oil, salt, and pepper.
3. In a resealable plastic bag, combine the dressing and the chicken pieces.
4. Seal the bag and toss to coat.
5. Refrigerate for at least 2 hours and up to a day, rotating the chicken pieces occasionally.
6. Place chicken in an oiled casserole dish and bake for 1 hour.
7. Cover the chicken with aluminum foil for the remainder of the cooking time if it browns too soon.
8. Place the chicken on a serving plate and serve.
9. Place the dish on a stove-top over and stir the chicken broth into the pan drippings.

10. Drizzle the juices over the chicken.
11. Serve the chicken with a lemon zest and parsley garnish.

NUTRITION:
Calories: 172 | Fat: 8 g | Carbohydrates: 9 g | Sugars: 1.6g | Protein: 15 g | Sodium: 321 mg

Olive Chicken

SERVINGS: 4
COOKING TIME: 120 MINUTES
DIFFICULTY: MODERATE

INGREDIENTS:
• 4 chicken thighs
• 1 tablespoon lemon juice
• 2 tablespoons olive oil
• 2 onions, thinly sliced
• 2 tablespoons lemon zest, grated
• 1 cup olives, pitted and sliced
• 3 garlic cloves, crushed
• ½ teaspoon ground ginger
• ¼ teaspoon saffron threads, crushed
• 1½ cups of chicken broth
• ¼ cup fresh parsley leaves, chopped
• ¼ cup fresh cilantro leaves, chopped
• ½ tablespoon salt
• Ground black pepper

INSTRUCTIONS:
1. Drizzle lemon juice over chicken and sprinkle with salt and black pepper.
2. In a Dutch oven, heat the oil over high heat and sear the chicken thighs for about 4 to 6 minutes on each side.
3. Bring the remaining ingredients to a boil, excluding the herbs.
4. Reduce to medium-low heat and cook for about 1 hour and 15 minutes.
5. Stir in the herbs and simmer for another 15 minutes.
6. Serve immediately.

NUTRITION:

Calories: 185 | Fat: 12 g | Carbohydrates: 15 g | Fiber: 6 g | Sodium: 389 mg | Protein: 23 g

Chicken, Vegetables & Mango

SERVINGS: 4
COOKING TIME: 35 MINUTES
DIFFICULTY: EASY

INGREDIENTS:
• 2 tablespoons almond oil
• 2 skinless (8 ounces), boneless chicken breasts, sliced
• 1 finely sliced red onion
• 1 mango, peeled, seeded, and diced
• 2 garlic cloves, minced
• 1 zucchini, sliced
• 1 cup mushrooms, sliced
• 3 tablespoons coconut aminos
• ¼ teaspoon red pepper flakes, crushed
• 1 bell pepper, diced
• Salt and ground black pepper
• ¼ cup cashews, toasted
• 2 tablespoons fresh ginger, chopped
• 1 broccoli bunch (cut into florets)

INSTRUCTIONS:
1. Melt the almond oil and sauté the chicken for about 5 minutes. Set aside.
2. Add the onion, garlic, and ginger to the same skillet and sauté for about 2 minutes.
3. Add the mango, broccoli, zucchini, and peppers; cook for 7 minutes.
4. Add chicken, sprouts, aminos, pepper flakes, salt, and pepper; cook for another 4 minutes.
5. Serve with cashews.

NUTRITION:

Calories: 184 | Fat: 4 g | Carbohydrates: 14 g | Fiber: 9 g | Sugars: 6 g | Protein: 27 g | Sodium: 260 mg

Creamy Baked Chicken

SERVINGS: 4
COOKING TIME: 25 MINUTES
DIFFICULTY: EASY

INGREDIENTS:
• ½ cup panko
• 1 tablespoon olive oil
• 2 medium boneless, skinless chicken breasts, sliced lengthways
• 1 teaspoon onion powder
• 1 teaspoon black pepper
• ¾ cup Greek yogurt
• ½ cup shredded low-fat cheddar cheese
• 1 teaspoon garlic powder

INSTRUCTIONS:
1. Arrange your chicken on a well-oiled rimmed baking sheet.
2. Dredge with Greek yogurt.
3. Mix the dry ingredients in a small mixing bowl and sprinkle on top of the chicken.
4. Bake for 12 minutes at 425 degrees.

NUTRITION:
Calories: 193 | Fat: 7 g | Sodium: 363 mg | Carbohydrates: 12 g | Fiber: 3 g | Sugars: 2 g | Protein: 20 g

Seared Chicken & Tomatoes

SERVINGS: 4
COOKING TIME: 25 MINUTES
DIFFICULTY: EASY

INGREDIENTS:
• 2 chicken breasts, cut lengthwise
• 1 cup cherry tomatoes, quartered
• 3 cloves garlic, minced
• 1 cup quinoa
• 1 tablespoon dill
• 1 teaspoon black pepper
• Juice of 1 lemon
• 1 cup reduced-fat feta cheese, crumbled
• 1 tablespoon vegetable oil
• 1 bell pepper, diced
• 1 teaspoon low-sodium salt
• 1 cucumber diced

INSTRUCTIONS:
1. Mix half the oil, garlic cloves, and basil with the chicken breasts in a zip-lock bag.
2. Bring the balsamic vinegar and honey to a boil.
3. In a small mixing dish, combine chopped tomatoes, remaining 2 garlic cloves, and 1/4 cup basil leaves; set aside.
4. In another pan, heat the remaining olive oil and brown chicken breasts for 3 minutes on each side.
5. Drizzle ¼ cup tomato mixture and balsamic glaze over chicken breast halves.

NUTRITION:
Calories: 234 | Fat: 10 g | Sodium: 88 mg | Carbohydrates: 19 g | Fiber: 6 g | Sugars: 3 g | Protein: 21 g

Sheet Pan Fajitas

SERVINGS: 4
COOKING TIME: 40 MINUTES
DIFFICULTY: MODERATE

INGREDIENTS:
- 8 corn tortillas
- 2 tablespoons olive oil
- 1 onion, sliced
- 3 cloves garlic, minced
- 2 bell peppers, sliced thin
- 1 teaspoon low-sodium salt
- 2 limes, divided
- 1 tablespoon chili powder
- ½ cup Greek yogurt
- ¾ teaspoon paprika
- 1 teaspoon cayenne
- 2 boneless, skinless chicken breasts, sliced thin
- ¾ tablespoon cumin

INSTRUCTIONS:
1. Drizzle olive oil over chicken, onions, peppers, and garlic on a rimmed baking sheet.
2. Whisk chili powder, cumin, cornstarch, paprika, salt, and cayenne pepper and season chicken and the vegetables.
3. Bake the chicken and vegetables for 25 minutes at 425º F.
4. Meanwhile, zest and juice a lime, then combine with Greek yogurt.
5. Serve the fajitas with a side of Greek yogurt and lime wedges.

NUTRITION:
Calories: 240 | Fat: 5 g | Sodium: 236 mg | Carbohydrates: 23 g | Fiber: 6 g | Sugars: 4 g | Protein: 18 g

Chicken Cauliflower Casserole

SERVINGS: 8
COOKING TIME: 90 MINUTES
DIFFICULTY: HARD

INGREDIENTS:
- 2 tablespoons coconut oil
- 2-2½ pounds bone-in chicken thighs and drumsticks
- Salt and ground black pepper
- 2 garlic cloves, crushed
- 1 teaspoon ground cinnamon
- ½ teaspoon ground turmeric
- 3 carrots, peeled and sliced
- 1 teaspoon paprika
- 2 teaspoons cumin powder
- ¼ teaspoon cayenne pepper
- 28-ounce can of tomatoes with liquid
- 2 tablespoons ginger, chopped
- 1 teaspoon of salt
- 1 head cauliflower, shredded
- 1 onion, chopped
- 1 teaspoon coriander powder
- 1 bell pepper, sliced
- 1 lemon, thinly sliced
- Fresh parsley, crumbled

INSTRUCTIONS:
1. Preheat your oven to 375° F.
2. Melt 1 tablespoon coconut oil and brown chicken for 5 minutes per side. Set aside.
3. Sauté the carrot, onion, garlic, and ginger for about 4 minutes.
4. Add the spices and remaining coconut oil and stir.
5. Add the chicken, tomatoes, peppers, parsley, and salt and simmer

for about 3-5 minutes.
6. Layer the cauliflower rice on the bottom of a rectangular baking dish.
7. Spoon chicken mixture evenly over cauliflower rice and garnish with lemon wedges.
8. Bake for 1 hour.

NUTRITION:
Calories: 265 | Fat: 14 g | Carbohydrates: 19 g | Fiber: 8 g | Sodium: 213 mg | Sugars: 3 g | Protein: 20 g

SOUP, STEW, & CURRY RECIPES

SOUP, STEW, & CURRY RECIPES

Cream of Kale

SERVINGS: 4
COOKING TIME: 30 MINUTES
DIFFICULTY: EASY

INGREDIENTS:
• 2 tablespoons olive oil (extra-virgin)
• 1 onion, diced
• 4 cups kale
• 1 cup broccoli florets
• 6 cups unsalted vegetable broth
• 1 teaspoon garlic powder
• ½ teaspoons sea salt
• ¼ teaspoon black pepper, freshly ground
• Handful Microgreens
• Coconut milk

INSTRUCTIONS:
1. In a saucepan, heat the olive oil. Add onion and sauté until the onion is soft, about 5 minutes.
2. Mix in kale, broccoli, vegetable broth, garlic powder, salt, and pepper.
3. Simmer for 15 minutes, stirring periodically.
4. Blend everything until smooth.
5. Serve with microgreens, and coconut milk.

NUTRITION:
Calories: 109 | Fat: 2 g | Carbohydrates: 16 g | Sodium: 210 mg | Sugars: 6 g | Fiber: 12 g | Protein: 5 g

Coral Lentil & Swiss Chard Soup

SERVINGS: 4
COOKING TIME: 40 MINUTES
DIFFICULTY: MODERATE

INGREDIENTS:
• 2 tablespoons olive oil
• 1 medium onion, diced
• 2 carrots, diced
• ½ teaspoon ginger powder
• ½ teaspoon turmeric powder
• 2 minced big garlic cloves
• 1 teaspoon cumin powder
• ½ teaspoon red pepper flakes
• ½ teaspoons sea salt
• 15-ounce can of diced tomatoes
• 1 cup dried red lentils
• 2 liters of vegetable broth
• 1 bunch Swiss chard, coarsely chopped

INSTRUCTIONS:
1. In a soup or casserole dish, heat the oil.
2. Sauté onion and carrot for 7 minutes.
3. Add garlic, cumin, ginger, turmeric, chili flakes, and salt.
4. Add tomatoes and cook for 5 minutes.
5. Add the lentils and broth and bring to a boil, then reduce to low heat and cook, uncovered, for 10 minutes until lentils are cooked.
6. Cook for another 5 minutes, until the chard has wilted.
7. Season with salt and pepper to taste.
8. Serve with a wedge of lemon.

NUTRITION:
Calories: 108 | Fat: 2 g | Carbohydrates: 23 g | Fiber: 21 g | Protein:

16 g | Sodium: 91 mg

Stewed Cashew Vegetables

SERVINGS: 3
COOKING TIME: 45 MINUTES
DIFFICULTY: EASY

INGREDIENTS:
- 1½ cup broccoli florets
- 1½ cup cauliflower florets
- 2 tablespoons olive oil
- 1 big sliced onion
- ¼ teaspoon fresh ginger, grated
- 2 garlic cloves, minced
- 1 pinch Low-Sodium Salt
- 1 pinch black pepper
- 2 cups vegetable broth
- 1 pound cashews
- 1 teaspoon cumin powder
- 1 teaspoon cayenne pepper
- 1 tablespoon lemon juice, freshly squeezed
- 1 teaspoon fresh lemon zest, grated

INSTRUCTIONS:
1. Sauté the onion in oil for about 3 minutes.
2. Add the garlic, ginger, and spices.
3. Bring to a boil with 1 cup of broth.
4. Add the vegetables and boil again.
5. Cook, stirring periodically, for 15 to 20 minutes with the lid on.
6. Remove from heat after adding the lemon juice.
7. Serve hot with cashew nuts and lemon zest.

NUTRITION:
Calories: 125 | Fat: 2 g | Carbohydrates: 22 g | Fiber: 18 g | Sugars: 3 g | Protein: 13 g | Sodium: 127 mg

Chickpea and Vegetable Curry

SERVINGS: 6
COOKING TIME: 40 MINUTES
DIFFICULTY: MODERATE

INGREDIENTS:
- 15-ounce can of chickpeas, rinsed and drained
- ¼ cup onion, diced
- 4 garlic cloves, crushed
- 2-3 tablespoons of water
- 1 teaspoon olive oil
- ½ teaspoon ground coriander
- ½ teaspoon ground cumin
- ½ teaspoon ground turmeric
- ¼ teaspoon ground cardamom
- 1 piece of ginger, chopped
- ¼ teaspoon ground cinnamon
- ⅓ teaspoon cayenne pepper
- ½ cup coconut milk
- 3 tablespoons almond butter
- ¾ cup vegetable broth
- ½ cup zucchini, sliced
- ½ cup carrots, peeled and sliced
- ½ red bell pepper, seeded and sliced
- ¼ teaspoon red pepper flakes, crushed
- 1 pinch low-sodium salt
- 1 pinch black pepper
- ¼ cup fresh cilantro, chopped
- 1 teaspoon lime juice

INSTRUCTIONS:
1. Place the onion, ginger, garlic, and water in a blender and purée until smooth.

2. Heat the oil in a skillet and cook the spices for about 30 seconds.
3. Sauté for 9 minutes after adding the onion mixture.
4. Add coconut milk and almond butter and mix well.
5. Increase the heat to medium-high.
6. Stir in broth, chickpeas, vegetables, pepper flakes, salt, and pepper.
7. Simmer for 10 minutes and add the lime juice and cilantro.

NUTRITION:
Calories: 116 | Fat: 2 g | Carbohydrates: 21 g | Fiber: 24 g | Sugars: 5 g | Protein: 19 g | Sodium: 146 mg

DASH Diet-Friendly Bean and Broccoli Chili

SERVINGS: 2
COOKING TIME: 40 MINUTES
DIFFICULTY: EASY

INGREDIENTS:
- 1 bunch of spinach
- Himalayan Salt and freshly ground black pepper
- 2 tablespoons tomato purée
- 1 tablespoon olive oil
- 1 onion, chopped
- 1 garlic clove, crushed
- 1 red chili, thinly sliced
- ½ teaspoon ground cumin
- ½ teaspoon ground coriander
- 1 head of broccoli, chopped small
- 1 can of chopped tomatoes
- Wedges of lime, to serve
- ½ yeast free veg stock cube
- Dash Liquid Aminos
- 15 tablespoons can red kidney beans, drained

INSTRUCTIONS:
1. Heat stock and steam the onion and garlic.
2. Add the stock cube, tomatoes, tomato purée, chili, cumin, coriander, Aminos sauce, salt, and pepper.
3. Simmer for about 20 minutes.
4. Combine the kidney beans and fresh coriander in a mixing bowl and cook for another 9 minutes.
5. Top with raw broccoli and spinach, as well as avocado or olive oil.

NUTRITION:
Calories: 110 | Fat: 3 g | Sodium: 247 mg | Carbohydrates: 20 g |

Fiber: 28 g | Protein: 8 g

Lentil & Butternut Squash Stew

SERVINGS: 4
COOKING TIME: 45 MINUTES
DIFFICULTY: EASY

INGREDIENTS:
- 16 tablespoons brown lentils, soaked
- 2 brown onions
- 20 oz. wheat-free vegetable stock
- 4 carrots
- ½ butternut squash
- 1 sweet potato
- 2 white potatoes
- 1 stick of celery
- Handful fresh garden peas
- Handful watercress
- 2 tablespoons fresh dill
- 1 teaspoon tamari sauce

INSTRUCTIONS:
1. Bring stock and onions to a boil in a pan.
2. Add lentils, potatoes, squash, and carrot and simmer for 15 minutes.
3. Toss in the celery, fresh peas, leaves, and dill.

NUTRITION:
Calories: 97 | Protein: 6 g | Carbohydrates: 15 g | Fiber: 24 g | Sugars: 1 g | Fat: 1.3 g | Sodium: 172 mg

Fish Stew with Chili

SERVINGS: 4
COOKING TIME: 15 MINUTES
DIFFICULTY: EASY

INGREDIENTS:
• 1 onion, chopped
• 2 fennel bulbs, chopped
• 1 red chili, finely chopped
• 1 tin plum tomatoes
• 6 tablespoons olive oil
• 1 teaspoon fennel seeds, ground
• 2 cloves of garlic, crushed
• 1 lb. white fish fillet
• 3 oz. toasted almonds, ground
• 3 oz. vegetable stock
• ½ teaspoon sweet paprika powder
• 1 tablespoon fresh thyme leaves
• 1 teaspoon saffron strands
• 3 fresh bay leaves
• Quinoa and spring greens
• 1 lemon, cut into wedges

INSTRUCTIONS:
1. Steam onions, fennel, chili, crushed fennel seeds, and garlic.
2. Add paprika, thyme, saffron, bay leaves, and tomatoes.
3. Bring to a simmer with the vegetable stock.
4. Add the fish/tofu to the stew, along with the almonds.
5. Serve with greens, quinoa, and lemon wedges.

NUTRITION:
Calories: 137 | Protein 8 g | Carbohydrates: 24 g | Fiber: 14 g |
Sugars: 1.3 g | Fat: 3 g | Sodium: 231 mg

DASH Diet Chicken and Quinoa Soup

SERVINGS: 6
COOKING TIME: 30 MINUTES
DIFFICULTY: EASY

INGREDIENTS:
• 1 onion, chopped
• 4 cups fat-free, low-sodium chicken broth
• 1 tablespoon thyme, chopped
• 1 cup water
• 3 large garlic cloves, minced
• 1 carrot, sliced
• 1 teaspoon pepper
• 1 lb. boneless, skinless chicken breasts, cubed
• ½ cup uncooked quinoa
• 1 dried bay leaf
• 2 ounces sugar snap peas, sliced

INSTRUCTIONS:
1. Bring the chicken, broth, onion, water, carrot, garlic, thyme, bay leaf, and pepper to a boil.
2. Cover and simmer for 5 minutes.
3. Stir in the quinoa thoroughly.
4. Bake for 5 minutes at 350° F.
5. Stir in the peas thoroughly for 8 minutes.
6. Remove the bay leaf and serve.

NUTRITION:
Calories: 145 | Carbohydrates: 21 g | Protein: 18 g | Fat: 3 g | Sodium: 182 mg | Fiber: 14 g | Sugars: 2 g

Red Bean Stew from Jamaica

SERVINGS: 4
COOKING TIME: 50 MINUTES
DIFFICULTY: EASY

INGREDIENTS:
- 1 yellow onion, chopped
- 2 carrots, cut into slices
- ½ cup water
- 13.5-ounce can of coconut milk
- 2 garlic cloves, minced
- ¼ teaspoon black pepper
- 1 sweet potato, peeled and diced
- 3 cups cooked dark red kidney beans, drained and rinsed
- 1 tablespoon olive oil
- 1 teaspoon hot or mild curry powder
- 1 teaspoon dried thyme
- ¼ teaspoon ground allspice
- ½ teaspoon low-sodium salt
- 14.5-ounce can of diced tomatoes, drained

INSTRUCTIONS:
1. Heat the oil in a saucepan and cook the onion and carrots, about 4 minutes.
2. Add garlic, sweet potato, and red pepper followed by kidney beans, tomatoes, curry powder, thyme, allspice, salt, and black pepper.
3. Stir in the water, and simmer, covered, for 30 minutes.
4. Stir in the coconut milk right at the end.

NUTRITION:
Calories: 190 | Fat: 4 g | Sodium: 387 mg | Carbohydrates: 30 g | Fiber: 15 g | Protein: 12 g

Aubergine DASH Diet Chili

SERVINGS: 4
COOKING TIME: 30 MINUTES
DIFFICULTY: EASY

INGREDIENTS:
- 1 red onion, finely chopped
- Coconut or olive oil
- 1 aubergine cut into cubes
- 2 garlic cloves, crushed
- 5 small red chilies, chopped
- ½ teaspoons coriander powder
- 1 teaspoon of cumin powder
- 1 teaspoon of cinnamon powder
- 1 can of tomatoes
- 2 cups black beans, cooked
- Sea salt
- Freshly ground black pepper
- 2 serves of brown rice, quinoa, or couscous

INSTRUCTIONS:
1. Melt the coconut oil and fry the aubergines for 4 minutes. Set aside.
2. Sauté the onions and garlic, then add the chiles for 4 minutes.
3. Add the tomatoes, coriander, seasonings, and aubergine, and cook for 5 minutes.
4. Add the black beans and cook for 9 minutes.

NUTRITION:
Calories: 120 | Fat: 2 g | Sodium: 230 mg | Carbohydrates: 18 g | Fiber: 26 g | Protein: 12 g

Fall Pumpkin Soup

SERVINGS: 6
COOKING TIME: 60 MINUTES
DIFFICULTY: MODERATE

INGREDIENTS:
• 20 oz. pumpkin, peeled and chopped
• 2 cups of vegetable broth
• 1 teaspoon of cumin powder
• ½ cup coconut milk
• frying oil
• 1 tablespoon lemongrass, chopped
• 1 ginger, peeled and grated
• 2 kaffir lime leaves, chopped
• 1 teaspoon coriander seeds
• 1 red pepper, seeded and sliced
• 1 fresh turmeric, peeled and sliced
• Black pepper to taste
• 1 shallot, chopped
• 4 garlic cloves

INSTRUCTIONS:
1. Toss the squash in the oil before placing it on the baking sheet and roasting until golden brown.
2. In a pan, heat the oil and sauté the shallots until brown.
3. Add cumin and coriander.
4. Add the kaffir leaves, turmeric, ginger, lemongrass, and chili, and cook for another minute, stirring to avoid burning
5. Add the squash to the broth then cover and cook
6. Simmer for another 10 minutes.
7. Add the coconut milk and cook for 6 minutes.

NUTRITION:

Calories: 119 | Carbohydrates: 22 g | Protein: 6 g | Fat: 1.2 g | Sodium: 173 mg | Fiber: 23 g | Sugars: 2 g

Barley Vegetable Soup

SERVINGS: 6
COOKING TIME: 45 MINUTES
DIFFICULTY: EASY

INGREDIENTS:
• 1 cup carrots, chopped
• 1 clove of garlic, minced
• ¾ cup peeled barley
• Vegan parmesan, Grated
• 4 cups vegetable broth
• 1 cup celery, chopped
• 28-ounce can of tomato purée
• 15-ounce can of beans, drained and rinsed
• 2 cups kale, coarsely chopped
• 1 sprig of rosemary

INSTRUCTIONS:
1. Cook the onions, carrots, and celery with olive oil in a pan.
2. Add the rosemary, garlic, and barley.
3. Bring the broth to a boil, constantly stirring.
4. Reduce the heat to low, and cook for about 1 hour until the barley is cooked, then add the tomatoes and beans.
5. Serve with vegan parmesan.

NUTRITION:
Calories: 115 | Carbohydrates: 12 g | Protein: 7 g | Fat: 1.4 g | Fiber: 23 g | Sodium: 180 mg

Squash and Lentil Soup

SERVINGS: 4
COOKING TIME: 120 MINUTES
DIFFICULTY: EASY

INGREDIENTS:
• 8 cups of vegetable broth
• 1 large onion, diced
• 1 peeled and diced butternut squash
• 1 cup brown lentils
• 2 teaspoons minced garlic
• 1 bay leaf
• ½ teaspoon ground nutmeg
• 1 cup spinach, chopped
• ½ teaspoon of salt

INSTRUCTIONS:
1. Add all ingredients except spinach to your slow cooker and mix well.
2. Simmer for 80 minutes.
3. Remove the bay leaf.
4. Add chopped spinach and stir until softened.

NUTRITION:
Calories: 127 | Fat: 2 g | Carbohydrates: 23 g | Fiber: 34 g | Protein: 12 g | Sodium: 227 mg

PASTA & NOODLE RECIPES

PASTA & NOODLE RECIPES

Rosemary Pasta Shells Soup

SERVINGS: 4
COOKING TIME: 30 MINUTES
DIFFICULTY: EASY

INGREDIENTS:
- 2 teaspoons olive oil
- Pinch red pepper flakes
- ½ cup whole wheat pasta shells
- 1 shallot, finely diced
- 1 garlic clove, minced
- 14.5-ounce can of white beans
- 3 Cups Baby Spinach, cleaned and trimmed
- ⅛ teaspoon black pepper
- 4 cups fat-free chicken broth
- 1 teaspoon rosemary
- 14.5-ounce can of diced tomatoes

INSTRUCTIONS:
1. Preheat the oven to 350° F.
2. Heat the oil and cook garlic and shallot for 4 minutes.
3. Add the broth, tomatoes, beans, rosemary, and black and red pepper to taste.
4. Cook until they begin to boil.
5. Add the noodles.
6. Finally, stir in the spinach.

NUTRITION:
Calories: 208 | Fat: 3 g | Carbohydrates: 48 g | Protein: 9 g | Sodium: 383 mg

Farfalle Pasta with Mushrooms

SERVINGS: 4
COOKING TIME: 45 MINUTES
DIFFICULTY: MODERATE

INGREDIENTS:
• 1 lb. farfalle pasta, cooked
• Pinch Low-Sodium Salt and pepper to taste
• 2 zucchinis, quartered and sliced
• 8-ounce package of mushrooms, sliced
• ⅓ cup olive oil
• 1 clove of garlic, chopped
• 1 tablespoon paprika
• 1 tablespoon dried oregano
• ¼ cup butter
• 1 onion, chopped
• 1 tomato, chopped

INSTRUCTIONS:
1. Fry garlic, mushrooms, onion, and tomato in olive oil for 17 minutes.
2. Season with salt, pepper, paprika, and oregano.
3. Combine the vegetables and noodles in a mixing bowl.

NUTRITION:
Calories: 250 | Carbohydrates: 73 g | Fat: 4 g | Protein: 18 g | Sodium: 390 mg

Tortellini Salad with Spinach

SERVINGS: 2
COOKING TIME: 60 MINUTES
DIFFICULTY: EASY

INGREDIENTS:
- 9-ounce package of spinach and cheese
- 1 jar tortellini, cooked
- 4-ounce jar pesto
- ¼ cup halved, seeded, and sliced cucumber
- ¼ cup halved cherry tomatoes
- ¼ cup red onion, diced
- ½ Cup chopped mache

INSTRUCTIONS:
1. Place the cucumbers, tomatoes, onions, tortellini, and mache on top of the pesto in the jar.
2. Serve your salad right immediately or keep it refrigerated until ready to eat.

NUTRITION:
Calories: 286 | Fat: 4 g | Carbohydrates: 76 g | Protein: 12 g | Sodium: 327 mg

Egg Noodles with Croutons

SERVINGS: 4
COOKING TIME: 30 MINUTES
DIFFICULTY: EASY

INGREDIENTS:
- 12 oz. egg noodles, cooked
- 1 pinch low-sodium salt
- ½ cup unsalted butter
- ¼ teaspoon pepper
- 2 slices of white bread, torn

INSTRUCTIONS:
1. Heat the butter in a pan and cook the bread pieces until crisp.
2. Add salt and black pepper.
3. Combine the noodles and croutons in a serving bowl.

NUTRITION:
Calories: 216 | Fat: 5 g | Sodium: 208 mg | Carbohydrates: 67 g | Protein: 12 g

Snow Peas & Spaghetti

SERVINGS: 6
COOKING TIME: 60 MINUTES
DIFFICULTY: MODERATE

INGREDIENTS:
- 8 oz. spaghetti, cooked
- 1 lb. boneless skinless chicken breast
- 1 tablespoons cornstarch
- 2 cups fresh snow peas
- 4 tablespoons reduced-sodium soy sauce,
- 2 cups carrots, shredded
- 3 green onions, chopped
- 2 tablespoons sesame oil, divided
- ⅜ teaspoon ground ginger, minced
- ½ teaspoon crushed red pepper flakes
- 1 tablespoon canola oil
- 2 tablespoons white vinegar
- 1 tablespoon sugar

INSTRUCTIONS:
1. Whisk the sesame oil, cornstarch, and half the soy sauce in a zip-top bag along with the chicken.
2. Shake the bag to coat it and press it to seal it.
3. Set it aside for 20 minutes to absorb the flavors.
4. Mix the vinegar, sugar, remaining soy sauce, and sesame oil.
5. Heat the canola oil in a skillet and cook chicken for 8 minutes; add in the carrots, peas, green onions, ginger, and pepper flakes.
6. Combine chicken, vinegar sauce, and pasta; cook for 2 minutes before serving.

NUTRITION:
Calories: 287 | Fat: 8 g | Sodium: 405 mg | Carbohydrates: 79 g

Garlic and Sesame Noodles

SERVINGS: 4
COOKING TIME: 20 MINUTES
DIFFICULTY: EASY

INGREDIENTS:
• 1 pound brown rice spaghetti, cooked
• 1½ tablespoons toasted sesame oil
• 1 cup sliced green onions
• 7 garlic cloves, crushed
• ¼ cup soy sauce
• ¼ cup hazelnut sugar
• 2 tablespoons rice vinegar
• ½ teaspoon red pepper flakes
• Sesame seeds for garnish

INSTRUCTIONS:
1. Over low to medium heat, heat a skillet.
2. Pour in the sesame oil and once heated, stir in ¾ cup of green onions, garlic, and red pepper flakes.
3. Cook until garlic is lightly browned and fragrant, stirring frequently to avoid burning.
4. Add soy sauce, coconut sugar, and rice vinegar and stir to combine. Add the prepared, drained pasta and toss to coat with the sauce.
5. Cook for 2 minutes.
6. Serve topped with the remaining green onions and sesame seeds.

NUTRITION:
Calories: 235 | Carbohydrates: 47 g | Protein: 7 g | Fat: 4 g | Fiber: 6 g | Sodium: 302 mg

Tofu and Spinach Lasagne

SERVINGS: 4
COOKING TIME: 80 MINUTES
DIFFICULTY: EXPERT

INGREDIENTS:
• 2 handfuls of baby spinach
• 18 oz. soft silken tofu
• 1 aubergine, grilled
• Spelt Lasagne
• 1 courgette, grilled
• 8 Roma tomatoes, peeled
• A handful of fresh basil
• 1 red pepper, roasted and peeled
• 1 lemon
• 2 garlic cloves
• 1 red onion

INSTRUCTIONS:
1. Preheat the oven to 180 degrees Fahrenheit.
2. Blend the pepper, tomatoes, one garlic clove, and basil; set aside.
3. Blend tofu, the other garlic clove, lemon juice, and spinach to make a paste.
4. Make lasagne by layering the aubergine and courgette with the remaining tomatoes, tofu, spinach mixture, and a layer of lasagne.
5. Bake for 35 minutes.

NUTRITION:
Calories: 317 | Protein: 8 g | Carbohydrates: 84 g | Fiber: 4 g |
Sugars: 2 g | Fat: 7 g | Sodium: 434 mg

Salmon Fettuccini

SERVINGS: 6
COOKING TIME: 30 MINUTES
DIFFICULTY: EASY

INGREDIENTS:
• 12 ounces fresh salmon, cut into fillets
• Fresh basil
• Sea salt and pepper to taste
• 1 tablespoon clarified butter
• Juice one lemon, about 3 tablespoons
• 2 cloves garlic, minced
• 12 ounces spelt fettuccini, cooked
• 20 spinach leaves

INSTRUCTIONS:
1. Preheat the grill.
2. Gently rub salmon with salt & pepper, then grill for 6 minutes per side until the it readily flakes with a fork.
3. Heat lemon juice, and garlic with butter.
4. Toss pasta, garlic-butter sauce, spinach, and fresh basil in a serving dish.

NUTRITION:
Calories: 294 | Fat: 9 g | Sodium: 365 mg | Carbohydrates: 76 g | Fiber: 10 g | Protein: 23 g

Bell Pasta with Kidney Beans

SERVINGS: 4
COOKING TIME: 45 MINUTES
DIFFICULTY: EASY

INGREDIENTS:
- 3 Cups low fat, low chicken broth
- 1 cup whole tomatoes, chopped
- 1 cup seashell pasta
- 2 cups kidney beans, cooked
- 1 onion, chopped
- 2 teaspoon chopped fresh thyme
- ½ cup chopped spinach
- 1 red bell pepper, chopped
- 1 tablespoon olive oil
- 2 cloves garlic, minced
- 1 pinch ground black pepper to taste

INSTRUCTIONS:
1. Preheat a pot.
2. Heat oil and cook onion, bell pepper, and garlic for 3 minutes.
3. Mix in the broth, tomatoes, and beans and simmer for 20 minutes.
4. Mix in the thyme, spinach, and pasta and cook another 5 minutes.
5. Season with salt and pepper.

NUTRITION:
Calories: 204 | Fat: 4 g | Carbohydrates: 65 g | Protein: 9 g |
Sodium: 327 mg

Rigatoni Pasta Casserole

SERVINGS: 6
COOKING TIME: 90 MINUTES
DIFFICULTY: HARD

INGREDIENTS:
- 16-ounce rigatoni pasta, cooked
- ½ teaspoon garlic, minced
- 1 lb. ground sausage
- ¼ cup Romano cheese, grated
- 28-ounce can of Italian-style tomato sauce
- Parsley, to garnish
- 3 cups shredded mozzarella cheese
- 14-ounce can cannellini beans, drained and rinsed
- 1 teaspoon Italian seasoning

INSTRUCTIONS:
1. Preheat the oven to 350° F.
2. Using butter or oil, grease a casserole dish.
3. Cook garlic and sausages for 6 minutes and then add tomato sauce, beans, and Italian seasoning; simmer for 5 minutes.
4. Half of the sausage pasta mixture should be poured into the oiled casserole, followed by half of the mozzarella cheese. To make another layer, repeat the process.
5. Place a piece of foil on top of the dish and top it with Romano cheese.
6. Bake the rigatoni casserole for 26 minutes.

NUTRITION:
Calories: 305 | Fat: 12 g | Sodium: 546 mg | Carbohydrates: 92 g | Protein: 24 g

Vegetable DASH Diet Pasta

SERVINGS: 4
COOKING TIME: 30 MINUTES
DIFFICULTY: EASY

INGREDIENTS:
- ½ pack of vegetable or spelt pasta, cooked
- 1 courgette
- 1 medium broccoli
- 5 garlic gloves
- Chilies, diced
- 4 tomatoes
- A handful of basil leaves
- 1 tablespoon of olive oil
- Himalayan salt and black pepper

INSTRUCTIONS:
1. Heat the oil on a low, gentle heat, and sauté the garlic, basil, and chili for two minutes.
2. Add the remaining vegetables, which have been sliced to make them tiny and easy to cook.
3. Cook everything for another two minutes.

NUTRITION:
Calories: 160| Fat: 4 g | Sodium: 320 mg | Carbohydrates: 40 g | Fiber: 12 g | Protein: 9 g

Asparagus and Zucchini Pasta

SERVINGS: 4
COOKING TIME: 25 MINUTES
DIFFICULTY: EASY

INGREDIENTS:
• 1 zucchini
• 1 bunch asparagus, steamed
• 4 tomatoes, diced
• 7 oz. of rocket
• 12 basil leaves
• 2 cloves garlic
• ½ red onion, diced
• 4 servings of spelt pasta, cooked
• Olive oil

INSTRUCTIONS:
1. Combine onion and tomatoes with handfuls of rockets, and asparagus and set them aside.
2. Blend remaining ingredients until a smooth, light green sauce forms.
3. Toss the pasta with the sauce, divide it into bowls, and top with the tomato, red onion, asparagus, and rocket.

NUTRITION:
Calories: 160 | Fat: 4 g | Sodium: 189 mg | Carbohydrates: 58 g|
Fiber: 12 g | Protein: 6 g

Tomato & Cauliflower Spaghetti

SERVINGS: 4
COOKING TIME: 20 MINUTES
DIFFICULTY: EASY

INGREDIENTS:
- 1 tablespoon olive oil
- 9 tablespoons sun-blushed tomatoes, chopped
- 1 shallot, finely chopped
- 1 garlic clove, finely chopped
- Handful of rocket
- Handful of spinach
- Handful of cauliflower, chopped
- Handful chive, chopped
- ½ lemon, juice only
- 9 oz. spelt spaghetti, cooked

INSTRUCTIONS:
1. Heat the coconut oil and sauté the shallot, garlic, and tomatoes very gently.
2. Add the lemon juice.
3. Serve on top of the spaghetti.

NUTRITION:
Calories: 157 | Protein: 9 g | Carbohydrates: 64 g | Fiber: 12 g | Sugars: 1.5 g | Fat: 3 g | Sodium: 290 mg

VEGETABLE & LEAFY GREEN RECIPES

VEGETABLE & LEAFY GREEN RECIPES

DASH Diet Spinach and Potatoes

SERVINGS: 4
COOKING TIME: 120 MINUTES
DIFFICULTY: MODERATE

INGREDIENTS:
• 4 medium russet potatoes, washed
• 1 tablespoon oregano
• 1 tablespoon olive oil, extra-virgin
• 3 garlic cloves, crushed
• 1 teaspoon kosher salt
• ⅓ cup light cream cheese
• 1 cup onion, diced
• 1 teaspoon ground pepper
• 1-pound spinach, chopped
• 1 cup crumbled feta cheese

INSTRUCTIONS:
1. Preheat the oven to 400 degrees F.
2. Bake directly on the middle rack until tender, 50 to 60 minutes.
3. In a saucepan, heat the oil.
4. Add onion and cook until onion is soft, 3 minutes.
5. Add the spinach, garlic, and oregano.
6. Cook, stirring constantly, until the mixture is hot, about 4 minutes.
7. In a 9 x 13-inch skillet, arrange the potato skins.
8. Pulse the cream cheese, pepper, and salt using a hand blender.
9. Stir in spinach mixture and 1/2 cup feta. Fill each potato skin with about 3/4 cup filling. Sprinkle the remaining 1 tablespoon of feta on top.
10. Bake until topping is smoking and feta is golden brown, 25 to 35 minutes.

NUTRITION:

Calories: 147 | Protein: 15 g | Carbohydrates: 52 g | Fiber: 13 g | Fat: 2.3 g | Sodium: 290 mg

Brussels, Carrot & Greens

SERVINGS: 2
COOKING TIME: 20 MINUTES
DIFFICULTY: EASY

INGREDIENTS:
• 1 broccoli
• 2 carrots, sliced thin
• 6 brussels sprouts
• 2 cloves of garlic
• 1 teaspoon of caraway seeds
• ½ lemon
• Peel 1 lemon Olive oil

INSTRUCTIONS:
1. Steam all the vegetables for 8 minutes on low heat.
2. Sauté garlic with caraway seeds, lemon peel, lemon juice, and olive oil.
3. Add the carrot and Brussels sprouts.

NUTRITION:
Calories: 106 | Fat: 2 g | Sodium: 139 mg | Carbohydrates: 7 g | Fiber: 25 g | Protein: 7 g

Split Peas with Spinach

SERVINGS: 4
COOKING TIME: 20 MINUTES
DIFFICULTY: EASY

INGREDIENTS:
- 2 plum tomatoes, chopped
- ½ teaspoon turmeric
- 1cup yellow split peas, rinsed and drained
- 1 serrano chile, seeded and minced
- 4 cups water
- 1 teaspoon Low-Sodium Salt
- 1 teaspoon ground cumin
- 2 cups fresh baby spinach
- ¼ cup chopped fresh cilantro
- 1 tablespoon canola oil
- 2 garlic cloves, minced
- 1 tablespoon ginger, finely chopped
- ½ teaspoon ground coriander
- 2 teaspoons fresh lemon juice

INSTRUCTIONS:
1. Boil the split peas until soft, about 40 minutes.
2. Stir in the spinach, tomatoes; set aside.
3. Heat the oil in a skillet and cook the garlic, ginger, and chile for 1 minute.
4. Season with cumin, coriander, turmeric, and lemon juice.
5. Stir the mixture into the dal,
6. Serve.

NUTRITION:
Calories: 135 | Fat: 2 g | Sodium: 188 mg | Carbohydrates: 25 g | Fiber: 168 g | Sugars: 3 g | Protein: 16 g

Stir-Fried Vegetables & Rice

SERVINGS: 4
COOKING TIME: 25 MINUTES
DIFFICULTY: EASY

INGREDIENTS:
- 1 onion, chopped
- 1 carrot, chopped
- 2 teaspoons dry white wine
- 1 zucchini, chopped
- 2 tablespoons soy sauce
- 2 garlic cloves, minced
- ½ teaspoon turmeric
- 2 teaspoons grated fresh ginger
- 2 green onions, minced
- 2 tablespoons grape-seed oil
- 3 cups long-grain rice, cooked
- 1 cup peas
- 1 tablespoon toasted sesame oil

INSTRUCTIONS:
1. Heat the oil in a skillet and sauté the onion, carrot, and zucchini for about 5 minutes.
2. Mix in the garlic, ginger, and green onions, about 3 minutes.
3. Stir in the rice, peas, soy sauce, and wine, for about 5 minutes.
4. Drizzle with sesame oil.

NUTRITION:
Calories: 115 | Fat: 3 g | Sodium: 208 mg | Carbohydrates: 30 g |
Fiber: 27 g | Protein: 9 g

Aubergine, Potato & Chickpea

SERVINGS: 2
COOKING TIME: 25 MINUTES
DIFFICULTY: EASY

INGREDIENTS:
- 1 onion, peeled and finely sliced
- 1 teaspoon coriander
- 1 aubergine
- 1 potato
- 2 tablespoons coconut oil
- ½ teaspoons cumin
- 1 can chickpeas
- ¼ teaspoons turmeric
- Fresh coriander
SAUCE
- 1 onion, peeled and finely sliced
- 2 teaspoons ginger, peeled and grated
- ½ teaspoons cumin
- 6 whole cloves
- 16 oz. plum tomatoes
- ¼ teaspoons turmeric
- 2 tablespoons coconut oil
- 3 cloves garlic, crushed
- 1½ teaspoons salt
- 1 teaspoon red chili powder

INSTRUCTIONS:
1. Sauté onion and cumin seeds for 3 minutes.
2. Add the potato, aubergine, chickpeas, ground coriander, cumin, and turmeric.
3. Cook the onion, garlic, ginger, and cloves for sixty seconds and then add the chopped tomatoes, turmeric, and other spices.

4. Blend the sauces with a hand blender until they are roughly blended. After that, add the vegetables, coriander, water, salt, and pepper to taste.

NUTRITION:
Calories: 157 | Protein: 12 g | Carbohydrates: 43 g | Fiber: 17 g | Fat: 2 g | Sodium: 233 mg

Kale Slaw & Creamy Dressing

SERVINGS: 2
COOKING TIME: 10 MINUTES
DIFFICULTY: EASY

INGREDIENTS:
- ¼ cup sesame seeds
- 1 bell pepper
- ¼ cup sunflower seeds
- 1 red onion
- 1 bunch of kale
- 4 cups of red cabbage, shredded
- 1 piece of root ginger
- Fresh coriander
- 1 Serving cashew dressing

INSTRUCTIONS:
1. Toss all the ingredients together.

NUTRITION:
Calories: 92 | Fat: 3 g | Sodium: 209 mg | Carbohydrates: 12 g | Fiber: 25 g | Protein: 6 g

Broccoli Cauliflower Fry

SERVINGS: 4
COOKING TIME: 30 MINUTES
DIFFICULTY: EASY

INGREDIENTS:
- 4 broccoli florets
- 4 cauliflower florets
- 1 pepper
- Handful assorted sprouts
- 3 spring onions
- 1 garlic clove, chopped Liquid Aminos
- Wild/brown rice

INSTRUCTIONS:
1. Cook the rice in a vegetable stock that is yeast-free.
2. Fry the garlic and onion in a steamer for three minutes.
3. Toss in the remaining ingredients and simmer for a few minutes more.

NUTRITION:
Calories: 143 | Protein: 8 g | Carbohydrates: 25 g | Fiber: 17 g |
Sodium: 234 mg | Sugars: 2 g | Fat: 1.8 g

Veggie-Stuffed Tomatoes

SERVINGS: 2
COOKING TIME: 20 MINUTES
DIFFICULTY: EASY

INGREDIENTS:
• 1 tablespoon cold-pressed oil
• 2 tomatoes
• Half a small aubergine
• 1 onion
• ¼ of a courgette
• 1-2 cloves of garlic
• 1 pinch of sea salt and pepper
• 1 bunch of fresh spinach leaves

INSTRUCTIONS:
1. Preheat the oven to 325 degrees Fahrenheit.
2. Toss vegetables with spinach, salt, and pepper, and oil.
3. After that, place the tomatoes on top and scoop out the center. Combine the middle piece with the rest of the mixture and stir well.
4. Now you must carefully place everything back into the tomatoes.
5. Put the tomatoes in a large pan with about 80ml of water and cover it with a lid once you're sure there's nothing else that could fit into them.
6. Bake for 18 minutes.

NUTRITION:
Calories: 126 | Fat: 3 g | Sodium: 136 mg | Carbohydrates: 12 g | Fiber: 25 g | Protein: 8 g

DASH Diet Ratatouille

SERVINGS: 4
COOKING TIME: 30 MINUTES
DIFFICULTY: MODERATE

INGREDIENTS:
• 2 bunches of baby spinach
• 3 aubergines, skins removed and diced
• 6 Pitted black olives
• 3 courgettes, skins removed and diced
• 2 red peppers
• 5 tomatoes, diced
• 3 teaspoons thyme leaves
• 2 cloves of garlic
• Basil leaves
• Coriander seeds
• Drizzle extra virgin olive oil
• Pinch Himalayan salt & black pepper

INSTRUCTIONS:
1. In a skillet, heat a little olive or coconut oil and sauté one garlic bulb slowly.
2. Place the aubergine in a strainer and press with kitchen paper towels to remove any excess oil after cooking it all at once.
3. Heat more oil, then add the courgette and the other garlic.
4. Combine the remaining ingredients in a big pan and heat for 3 minutes.

NUTRITION:
Calories: 153 | Protein: 12 g | Carbohydrates: 19 g | Sodium: 237 mg | Fiber: 12 g | Fat: 2 g

Mushrooms & Spinach

SERVINGS: 3
COOKING TIME: 30 MINUTES
DIFFICULTY: EASY

INGREDIENTS:
- 1 teaspoon coconut oil
- 5-6 mushrooms, sliced
- 2 tablespoons olive oil
- 1 red onion, sliced
- 1 teaspoon fresh lemon zest, finely grated
- ¼ cup cherry tomatoes, sliced
- 1 pinch of ground nutmeg
- 3 cups fresh spinach, shredded
- 1 clove of garlic, minced
- ½ tablespoons fresh lemon juice
- 1 pinch low-sodium salt
- 1 pinch ground black pepper

INSTRUCTIONS:
1. Heat the coconut oil and sauté the mushrooms for about 4 minutes.
2. Sauté the onion in olive oil and for about 3 minutes.
3. Add the garlic, lemon zest and tomatoes, salt, and black pepper and cook for about 2-3 minutes, lightly crushing the tomatoes with a spatula.
4. Cook for about 3 minutes with the spinach.
5. Stir in mushrooms and lemon juice and remove from heat.

NUTRITION:
Calories: 158 | Fat: 2 g | Carbohydrates: 27 g | Fiber: 15 g | Sugars: 2 g | Protein: 11 g | Sodium: 191 mg

Citrus Spinach

SERVINGS: 4
COOKING TIME: 20 MINUTES
DIFFICULTY: EASY

INGREDIENTS:
• 2 tablespoons olive oil (extra-virgin)
• 4 cups fresh baby spinach
• 2 garlic cloves, crushed
• Juice of ½ orange
• The zest of ½ an orange
• ½ teaspoons sea salt
• ⅛ teaspoon black pepper, freshly ground

INSTRUCTIONS:
1. Heat the olive oil in a skillet.
2. Add spinach and cook for 3 minutes.
3. Garlic should be added now. Cook for 30 seconds while constantly stirring.
4. Add orange juice, orange zest, salt, and pepper.
5. Cook, stirring constantly until juices have evaporated, about 2 minutes.

NUTRITION:
Calories: 80 | Fat: 1.2 g | Carbohydrates: 7 g | Sugars: 5 g | Fiber: 22 g | Protein: 6 g | Sodium: 85 mg

Almond Balsamic Beans

SERVINGS: 4
COOKING TIME: 25 MINUTES
DIFFICULTY: EASY

INGREDIENTS:
• 2 tablespoons ground almonds
• 1 pound green beans
• 1 tablespoon olive oil
• 1½ tablespoons balsamic vinegar

INSTRUCTIONS:
1. Steam the green beans with olive oil and balsamic vinegar.
2. Add the almonds just before serving.

NUTRITION:
Calories: 116 | Fat: 1.7 g | Carbohydrates: 12 g | Sodium: 83 mg | Fiber: 26 g| Protein: 9 g

Turmeric Roasted Cauliflower

SERVINGS: 4
COOKING TIME: 30 MINUTES
DIFFICULTY: EASY

INGREDIENTS:
• 8 cups cauliflower florets
• 3 tablespoons olive oil (extra-virgin)
• ½ teaspoon cumin powder
• ½ teaspoon of salt
• 2 teaspoons turmeric powder
• 2 teaspoons lemon juice
• ½ teaspoon black pepper
• 2 large garlic cloves, crushed

INSTRUCTIONS:
• Preheat the oven to 425 degrees Fahrenheit.
• Whisk together oil, turmeric, cumin, salt, pepper, and garlic in a bowl.
• Add cauliflower and move to a rimmed baking sheet.
• Roast until golden brown and tender.
• Drizzle the lemon juice on top.

NUTRITION:
Calories: 105 | Protein: 7 g | Carbohydrates: 8 g | Fiber: 26 g | Sugars: 1.6 g | Fat: 1.2 g | Sodium: 139 mg

DESSERT RECIPES

DESSERT RECIPES

Assorted Berry Granita

SERVINGS: 4
COOKING TIME: 300 MINUTES
DIFFICULTY: EASY

INGREDIENTS:
• ½ cup fresh strawberries, peeled and sliced
• ½ cup of fresh raspberries
• ½ cup of fresh blueberries
• ½ cup fresh blackberries
• 1 tablespoon of maple syrup
• 1 tablespoon fresh lemon juice
• 1 cup ice cubes, crushed

INSTRUCTIONS:
1. Place berries, maple syrup, lemon juice, and ice cubes in a high-speed blender and blend on high speed until smooth.
2. Transfer the berry mixture to an 8 x 8-inch baking dish, spread evenly, and freeze for at least 30 minutes.
3. Take out of the freezer and stir the granita completely with a fork.
4. Freeze for 2-3 hours, stirring every 30 minutes.

NUTRITION:
Calories: 156 | Fat: 2 g | Carbohydrates: 11 g | Fiber: 8 g | Sugars: 7 g | Protein: 3 g | Sodium: 78 mg

Vegan Unsweetened Pumpkin Ice Cream

SERVINGS: 6
COOKING TIME: 270 MINUTES
DIFFICULTY: EASY

INGREDIENTS:
- 15 ounces home-made pumpkin purée
- ½ cup dates, pitted and chopped
- 2 cans (14 ounces) of unsweetened coconut milk
- ½ teaspoon organic vanilla extract
- 1½ teaspoons pumpkin pie spice
- ½ teaspoon ground cinnamon

INSTRUCTIONS:
1. Blend all ingredients until smooth.
2. Freeze for up to 2 hours.
3. Pour into an ice cream maker and process.
4. Freeze for another 2 hours before serving.

NUTRITION:
Calories: 196 | Fat: 1.3 g | Carbohydrates: 14 g | Fiber: 12 g | Sugars: 9 g | Protein: 5 g | Sodium: 62 mg

Frozen Fruity Dessert

SERVINGS: 6
COOKING TIME: 60 MINUTES
DIFFICULTY: EASY

INGREDIENTS:
• 14-ounce can of coconut milk
• 1 cup frozen pineapple chunks, thawed
• 4 cups frozen banana slices, thawed
• 2 tablespoons fresh lime juice
• 1 pinch of salt

INSTRUCTIONS:
1. Line a glass casserole dish with plastic wrap.
2. Blend all ingredients until smooth.
3. Fill the prepared casserole dish equally with the mixture.
4. Before serving, freeze for about 40 minutes.

NUTRITION:
Calories: 175 | Fat: 1.6 g | Carbohydrates: 12 g | Sodium: 98 mg | Fiber: 13 g | Sugars: 7 g | Protein: 4 g

Avocado Pudding

SERVINGS: 4
COOKING TIME: 160 MINUTES
DIFFICULTY: EASY

INGREDIENTS:
• 2 cups bananas, peeled and chopped
• 2 ripe avocados, peeled and chopped
• 1 teaspoon lime zest, finely grated
• 1 teaspoon lemon zest, finely grated
• ½ cup fresh lime juice
• ¼ cup honey
• ¼ cup almonds, chopped
• ½ cup lemon juice

INSTRUCTIONS:
1. Blend all ingredients until smooth.
2. Pour the mousse into 4 serving glasses.
3. Refrigerate for 2 hours before serving.
4. Garnish with nuts and serve.

NUTRITION:
Calories: 142 | Fat: 1.5 g | Carbohydrates: 9 g | Fiber: 13 g | Sugars: 7 g | Protein: 4 g | Sodium: 65 mg

DASH Diet-Friendly Pumpkin Cream

SERVINGS: 6
COOKING TIME: 90 MINUTES
DIFFICULTY: MODERATE

INGREDIENTS:
- 1 cup pumpkin
- 1 teaspoon ground cinnamon
- ¼ teaspoon ground ginger
- 2 pinches of freshly grated nutmeg
- 2 organic eggs
- 1 cup coconut milk
- 8-10 drops of liquid stevia
- 1 teaspoon organic vanilla extract

INSTRUCTIONS:
1. Preheat your oven to 350º F.
2. Mix the pumpkin and spices in a bowl.
3. In a separate bowl, whisk the eggs.
4. Mix in the other ingredients until fully combined.
5. Add egg mixture to pumpkin mixture and stir until well blended.
6. Transfer the mixture to 6 ramekins.
7. place the mussels in a casserole,
8. Add water to the casserole around the ramekins.
9. Bake for at least 1 hour.

NUTRITION:
Calories: 150 | Fat: 2.1 g | Carbohydrates: 25 g | Fiber: 7 g | Sugars: 5 g | Protein: 6 g | Sodium: 65 mg

SERVINGS: 6
COOKING TIME: 40 MINUTES
DIFFICULTY: EASY

INGREDIENTS:
• 18 ounces fresh strawberries, peeled and puréed
• ¼ cup raw honey
• 5 organic egg whites
• 4 teaspoons fresh lemon juice

INSTRUCTIONS:
1. Preheat your oven to 350° F.
2. In a bowl, combine the strawberry purée, 3 tablespoons of honey, 2 eggs, and the lemon juice, and pulse until fluffy and light.
3. In another bowl, add the remaining proteins and beat until fluffy.
4. Mix in the remaining honey.
5. Gently stir the Proteins into the strawberry mixture.
6. Transfer the mixture evenly into 6 ramekins and onto a baking sheet.
7. Cook for about 10-12 minutes.
8. Remove from oven and serve immediately.

NUTRITION:
Calories: 126 | Fat: 1.5 g | Carbohydrates: 13 g | Fiber: 8 g | Sugars: 15 g | Protein: 8 g | Sodium: 90 mg

Pumpkin Pie

SERVINGS: 8
COOKING TIME: 360 MINUTES
DIFFICULTY: HARD

INGREDIENTS:
FOR THE CRUST
- 2½ cups almonds
- 1 teaspoon baking powder
- 1 pinch of salt
- 2 tablespoons almond oil, melted
FOR FILLING
- 1 can (15 ounces) of unsweetened pumpkin purée
- 1 tablespoon arrowroot powder
- ½ teaspoon ground nutmeg
- 3 tablespoons honey
- ½ teaspoon ground cinnamon
- ¼ teaspoon ground ginger
- 3 eggs, beaten
- ¼ teaspoon ground cardamom
- ¼ teaspoon ground cloves
- 1 pinch of salt
- 1 cup coconut milk

INSTRUCTIONS:
1. Preheat your oven to 350° F.
2. In a food processor, pulse the nuts, baking soda, and salt.
3. Add the almond oil and pulse until well blended.
4. Place crust mixture in a 9-inch cake pan.
5. Place the cake tin on a baking sheet and bake for about 15 minutes.
6. Put all the filling ingredients in a bowl and mix well.
7. Remove the crust from the oven.

8. Spoon the mixture into the crust.
9. Bake for about 50 minutes.
10. Freeze about 3 hours before serving.

NUTRITION:
Calories: 181 | Fat: 2.3 g | Carbohydrates: 28 g | Fiber: 7 g | Sugars: 12 g | Protein: 8 g | Sodium: 110 mg

Spicy Zucchini Brownies

SERVINGS: 4
COOKING TIME: 60 MINUTES
DIFFICULTY: EASY

INGREDIENTS:
- 1½ cups zucchini, grated
- 1 cup dark chocolate chips
- 1 egg
- 1 cup almond butter
- ¼ cup raw honey
- 1 teaspoon baking powder
- 1 teaspoon ground cinnamon
- ½ teaspoon ground nutmeg
- 1 teaspoon vanilla extract

INSTRUCTIONS:
1. Preheat your oven to 350° F and grease a baking dish.
2. Combine all of the ingredients in a bowl and pour the mixture into the prepared pan.
3. Bake for about 40 minutes.
4. Cut into squares and serve.

NUTRITION:
Calories: 116 | Fat: 1.8 g | Carbohydrates: 12 g | Fiber: 7 g | Sugars: 9 g | Protein: 5 g | Sodium: 83 mg

Pineapple Upside-Down Cake

SERVINGS: 6
COOKING TIME: 90 MINUTES
DIFFICULTY: HARD

INGREDIENTS:
- 5 tablespoons raw honey
- 2 slices of fresh pineapple
- 15 fresh sweet cherries
- 1 cup almond flour
- ½ teaspoon baking powder
- 2 organic eggs
- 3 tablespoons almond oil, melted
- 1 teaspoon organic vanilla extract

INSTRUCTIONS:
1. Preheat your oven to 350° F.
2. In an 8-inch round cake pan, evenly spread about 1½ tablespoons of honey.
3. Arrange the pineapple slices and 15 cherries on top of the honey.
4. Bake for about 15 minutes.
5. Combine almond flour and baking powder in a bowl.
6. In another bowl, add the eggs and the rest of the honey and beat until creamy.
7. Add the almond oil and vanilla extract and beat until well combined.
8. In a bowl, combine the flour, baking powder, and salt.
9. Remove the cake pan from the oven.
10. Over the pineapple and cherries, evenly distribute the flour mixture.
11. Bake for 35 minutes.
12. Remove from the oven and allow to cool for 10 minutes.
13. Invert the cake onto a serving plate.

NUTRITION:
Calories: 185 | Fat: 1.4 g | Carbohydrates: 16 g | Fiber: 8 g | Sugars: 5 g | Protein: 6 g | Sodium: 237 mg

Crusty Peanut Butter Bars

SERVINGS: 4
COOKING TIME: 60 MINUTES
DIFFICULTY: MODERATE

INGREDIENTS:
CRUST
- ½ teaspoon Cinnamon
- 1 pinch of salt
- 1 cup Almond Flour
- 1 tablespoon Erythritol
- ¼ cup butter, melted
FUDGE
- ¼ cup Erythritol
- ¼ cup Heavy Cream
- ⅛ teaspoon Xanthan Gum
- ¼ cup butter, melted
- ½ cup Peanut Butter
- ½ teaspoon Vanilla Extract
TOPPING
- ¾ cup Chocolate, Chopped

INSTRUCTIONS:
1. Preheat the oven to 400 degrees Fahrenheit.
2. Mix almond flour with half of the melted butter followed by erythritol and cinnamon.
3. Press into a lined baking dish and bake for 10 minutes.
4. Blend all of the fudge ingredients and spread up the sides of the baking dish.
5. Top your bars with chopped chocolate just before cooling.
6. Remove the bars by peeling the parchment paper out once they have cooled.

NUTRITION:
Calories: 195 | Fat: 1.8 g | Sodium: 214 mg | Carbohydrates: 16 g | Protein: 4 g

Pumpkin and Date Ice Cream

SERVINGS: 6
COOKING TIME: 300 MINUTES
DIFFICULTY: EASY

INGREDIENTS:
- ½ teaspoon vanilla extract
- 15 ounces pumpkin purée
- 2 cans of unsweetened coconut milk
- ½ cup dates, pitted and chopped
- ½ teaspoon ground cinnamon
- 1½ teaspoons pumpkin pie spice

INSTRUCTIONS:
1. Blend all the ingredients until smooth.
2. Freeze for up to 2 hours.
3. Pour the mixture into an ice cream machine halfway and process.
4. Freeze the ice cream for around 1 to 2 hours before serving it in an airtight container.

NUTRITION:
Calories: 193 | Fat: 2 g | Carbohydrates: 15 g | Fiber: 6 g | Sugars: 12 g | Protein: 3 g | Sodium: 85 mg

DASH Diet Pumpkin Ramekin

SERVINGS: 6
COOKING TIME: 90 MINUTES
DIFFICULTY: EASY

INGREDIENTS:
- 9 drops of liquid stevia
- 1 cup canned pumpkin
- 1 teaspoon cinnamon powder
- 1 teaspoon vanilla extract
- ¼ teaspoon ginger powder
- 1 pinch of salt
- 2 teaspoons of nutmeg powder
- 2 eggs, beaten
- 1 cup coconut milk

INSTRUCTIONS:
1. Preheat your oven to 350° F.
2. Mix the pumpkin and spices.
3. Mix eggs with other ingredients.
4. Add egg mixture to pumpkin mixture and stir until well blended.
5. Transfer the mixture to 6 ramekins.
6. Pour water around the ramekins.
7. Bake for at least 1 hour.

NUTRITION:
Calories: 210 | Fat: 3.8 g | Carbohydrates: 16 g | Fiber: 5 g | Sugars: 9 g | Protein: 8 g | Sodium: 175 mg

SMOOTHIE RECIPES

SMOOTHIE RECIPES

Berry Cleanser Smoothie

SERVINGS: 2
COOKING TIME: 10 MINUTES
DIFFICULTY: EASY

INGREDIENTS:
- 3 Swiss chard leaves, stems removed
- ¼ cup frozen cranberries
- 1 cup of raspberries
- 2 pitted Medjool date
- 2 tablespoons ground flaxseed
- 1 cup of water

INSTRUCTIONS:
1. Add all the ingredients and blend till smooth.

NUTRITION:
Calories: 146 | Fat: 1.2 g | Sodium: 46 mg | Carbohydrates: 9 g |
Fiber: 16 g | Sugars: 9 g | Protein 2.5 g

Green Twist Smoothie

SERVINGS: 2
COOKING TIME: 10 MINUTES
DIFFICULTY: EASY

INGREDIENTS:
• 1 cup kale, stems removed
• 1 cup dandelion greens
• 1 orange, peeled, seeds removed
• 2 cups strawberries
• 2 kiwis, peeled and chopped
• ½ tablespoon lemon juice
• ½ cup water

INSTRUCTIONS:
1. Add all the ingredients except the purified water to a blender.
2. Add water and ice to the desired consistency. Process until smooth.

NUTRITION:
Calories: 70 | Fat 0.5 g | Carbohydrates: 7 g | Protein: 3 g | Sodium: 39 mg

Pina Colada Green Smoothie

SERVINGS: 2
COOKING TIME: 10 MINUTES
DIFFICULTY: EASY

INGREDIENTS:

• 2 cups spinach leaves
• 1 cup fresh pineapple, chopped
• 1 cup blueberries
• 1 tablespoon ground flaxseed
• 1 cup coconut water
• ½ cup of water

INSTRUCTIONS:

1. Add all the ingredients except the purified water to a blender.
2. Add water to taste. Process until smooth.

NUTRITION:

Calories: 104 | Carbohydrates: 4 g | Protein: 8 g | Fat: 1 g | Sodium: 45 mg

Watercress Cranberry Smoothie

SERVINGS: 2
COOKING TIME: 10 MINUTES
DIFFICULTY: EASY

INGREDIENTS:
• 2 cups watercress
• 1 cup of pineapple
• 1 ripe banana, sliced
• 1 orange, peeled and chopped
• 1 pitted Medjool date (optional)
• 1 tablespoon powdered wheatgrass
• Purified water

INSTRUCTIONS:
1. Add all the ingredients except the purified water to a blender.
2. Add water for desired consistency.
3. Process until smooth.

NUTRITION:
Calories: 98 | Fat: 1 g | Carbohydrates: 5 g | Protein: 4 g | Sodium: 46 mg

Grape Berry Smoothie

SERVINGS: 2
COOKING TIME: 10 MINUTES
DIFFICULTY: EASY

INGREDIENTS:
• 2 cups fresh baby spinach, stems removed and chopped
• ½ cup seedless green grapes
• 1 cup raspberries
• 1 Medjool date (soften/soaked)
• 2 tablespoons chia seeds
• 1 teaspoon cinnamon powder
• ½ cup of water

INSTRUCTIONS:
1. Add all the ingredients except the purified water to a blender.
2. Add water to desired consistency. Process until smooth.

NUTRITION:
Calories: 82 | Fat: 0.7 g | Carbohydrates: 4 g | Protein: 2.5 g |
Sodium: 31 mg

Smooth Swiss Chia Smoothie

SERVINGS: 2
COOKING TIME: 10 MINUTES
DIFFICULTY: EASY

INGREDIENTS:
- ½ cup fresh parsley
- 1½ cups Swiss chard, chopped
- 2 ripe peaches or nectarines, stone removed and chopped
- 1 Medjool date (soak and soft)
- 1 tablespoon chia seeds
- ½ cup of water

INSTRUCTIONS:
1. Blend all ingredients until smooth.
2. Add water to desired consistency. Process until smooth.

NUTRITION:
Calories: 118 | Fat: 1.2 g | Carbohydrates: 9 g | Protein: 3 g | Sodium: 38 mg

CONCLUSION

You may find that food tastes different when you reduce your intake of processed, high-sodium foods. Your palate may need some time to adapt, but once it happens, you may realize that you like the DASH diet more than your previous eating habits. I hope this cookbook's delectable dishes will make the transition easier for you.

30-DAY MEAL PLAN

DAY	BREAKFAST	LUNCH	DINNER	SNACK / DESSERT
1	Blueberry Cinnamon Breakfast Bake	Mixed Green Salad with Beets	Barley Vegetable Soup	Tortilla Chips
2	Cinnamon Quinoa with Peach & Pecan	Spinach, Shrimp & Tangerine Bowl	Rigatoni Pasta Casserole	Frozen Fruity Dessert
3	Nutmeg-Spiced Quinoa Porridge	Split Peas with Spinach	Sea Bass with Vegetables	Strawberry Soufflé
4	Nut and Seed Granola	Snow Peas & Spaghetti	Sheet Pan Fajitas	Ham and Cheese Stromboli
5	Quick Oats with Coconut Milk	DASH Diet Spinach and Potatoes	Almond Balsamic Beans	DASH Diet Pumpkin Ramekin
6	Spicy Sweet Potato Breakfast Bowl	Roasted Lemon Herb Chicken	Vegetable DASH Diet Pasta	Olive Pizza Bombs
7	Cinnamon Chia Pudding	Farro Salad with Sweet Pea Pesto	Black Pepper Peach and Salmon	Cocoa Peanut Butter Bombs
8	Apple-Cinnamon	Low-Sodium Salad with	DASH Diet Chicken and	Pizza Breadsticks

	Chia	Capers	Quinoa Soup	
9	Apple Almond Coconut Bowl	Mango, Jalapeño & Bean Salad	Seared Chicken & Tomatoes	Corndog Muffins
10	Cinnamon Quinoa with Peach & Pecan	Mixed Green Salad with Beets	Sheet Pan Fajitas	Mini Portobello Pizza
11	Pecan Porridge with Banana	Veggie-Stuffed Tomatoes	Crusted Salmon with Dill	Avocado Pudding
12	Pork Cracklings with Eggs	DASH Diet Ratatouille	Chicken Cauliflower Casserole	Tofu and Capers Pizza
13	DASH Diet-Friendly Pumpkin Waffles	Aubergine, Potato & Chickpea	Paprika Salmon	Jalapeño Popper Bombs
14	Quick Oats with Coconut Milk	Rosemary Pasta Shells Soup	Mushrooms & Spinach	Tortilla Chips
15	Spicy Sweet Potato Breakfast Bowl	Roman Tuna Salad	Bell Pasta with Kidney Beans	Rotisserie Chicken Pizza
16	Italian Pizza Waffles	Mixed Green Salad with Beets	Orange Poached Salmon	Neapolitan Bombs
17	Protein Almond Muesli	Hearty Cauliflower Rice with Chicken	Red Bean Stew from Jamaica	Crusty Peanut Butter Bars

18	Paleo Porridge with Banana	Spicy Turkey Stir Fry	Turmeric Roasted Cauliflower	Corndog Muffins
19	Quick Oats with Coconut Milk	Tortellini Salad with Spinach	Creamy Baked Chicken	Spicy Zucchini Brownies
20	Apple-Cinnamon Chia	Garlic and Sesame Noodles	Honey & Amino Glazed Salmon	Cocoa Peanut Butter Bombs
21	Cinnamon Millet Porridge	Black Pepper Salmon with Yogurt	Rotisserie Chicken Pizza	Pina Colada Green Smoothie
22	Pork Cracklings with Eggs	Egg Noodles with Croutons	DASH Diet Chicken and Quinoa Soup	Avocado Pudding
23	Pecan Porridge with Banana	Spinach, Shrimp & Tangerine Bowl	Prawns with Asparagus	DASH Diet Pumpkin Ramekin
24	Apple Almond Coconut Bowl	DASH Diet Ratatouille	Fruit Prawn Curry	Pineapple Upside-Down Cake
25	Protein Almond Muesli	Stir-Fried Vegetables & Rice	Almond Balsamic Beans	Tofu and Capers Pizza
26	Italian Pizza Waffles	Mixed Green Salad with Beets	Orange Poached Salmon	Frozen Fruity Dessert
27	Spicy Sweet Potato Breakfast	Aubergine, Potato & Chickpea	Barley Vegetable Soup	Tortilla Chips

	Bowl			
28	Apple-Cinnamon Chia	Farfalle Pasta with Mushrooms	Paprika Salmon	Strawberry Soufflé
29	DASH Diet-Friendly Pumpkin Waffles	Low-Sodium Salad with Capers	Chicken Cauliflower Casserole	Spicy Zucchini Brownies
30	Apple Almond Coconut Bowl	Roman Tuna Salad	Almond Balsamic Beans	Jalapeño Popper Bombs

Made in the USA
Las Vegas, NV
07 January 2025

16015906R00129